Praise for

Mone_y

A *Publishers Weekly* Top 10 Selection in Business & Economics

"Jacob Goldstein is a lucid, entertaining explainer of all things economic."
—Ira Glass, host and executive producer of *This American Life*

"A sweeping new history....*Money* is fast-paced and chatty: We meet all the characters an academic book would include, their ideas and innovations blended with scandal and gossip to propel the story along. The effect is a history of currency full of astonishing tales you might tell a friend in the pub....This story gets to the heart of why money matters....*Money* should be required reading for every financial regulator....*Money* is great preparation for turbulent times: a vibrant and accessible grounding in how the evolution of cash—organic, random, and social—really works."
—*The New York Times*

"Jacob Goldstein makes the complexities of economics and monetary policy not just comprehensible, but also genuinely fascinating. Charting the history of money becomes a lens through which to understand human history, and how we arrived at now."
—John Green, #1 *New York Times* bestselling author of *Turtles All the Way Down* and *The Fault in Our Stars*

"Jacob Goldstein of *Planet Money* has a remarkable gift for making complicated economic issues beguilingly simple. He has written a wonderfully entertaining, freewheeling history of money, told with all the verve and wit and smart insights that have made his NPR show such a success."
—Liaquat Ahamed, author of Pulitzer Prize winner *Lords of Finance: The Bankers Who Broke the World*

"With shrewd observations and snappy anecdotes, Goldstein...shows how currency may be humanity's most successful fiction."
—*The New York Times* (Editors' Choice)

"This is largely an optimistic book…money might be the one thing that we all still believe in…. There's very little moralizing in [the] book."

—NPR *Morning Edition*

"It's no surprise that money has taken us on some wild rides over the centuries. In *Money*, Goldstein invites readers along for those adventures, serving as a first-rate tour guide throughout."

—*Columbia* magazine

"It is rare for a work on a subject so fraught with interpretation and misinterpretation to be both funny and accessible, beautiful and conversational, but Goldstein's *Money* hits the bullseye in every respect. It made me look at my wallet and its musty contents with fresh eyes. A must-read."

—Gary Shteyngart, author of the *New York Times* bestsellers *Little Failure* and *Super Sad True Love Story*

"Certainly one of the most entertaining [books about the history of currency]…. Jacob Goldstein covers over five millennia, including witty, incisive, and sometimes surprising takes."

—*Reuters*

"Goldstein is a master storyteller who weaves an intriguing tale of how money and economic systems rose, fell, and rose again. In his hands, money disappears and the personalities and motives of centuries-old influencers emerge in vivid detail to paint a picture of the history that has given us our current monetary system."

—Betsey Stevenson, professor of public policy and economics at the University of Michigan

"[*Money* is] jaunty, comedic, short, and informative."

—*The Gist* with Mike Pesta

"Thoroughly researched but thoroughly entertaining…told as a series of stories by one of radio's great storytellers."

—*Radio Spectrum*

"A brisk, brightly told history…. Goldstein deftly clarifies economic concepts…. An informative primer from a genial guide."

—*Kirkus Reviews*

"Goldstein's entertaining storytelling style makes complicated ideas clear and engaging. *Money* is a must-read for all those who've ever wondered what their paycheck actually means."

—*Booklist* (starred review)

Money

The True Story of a Made-Up Thing

Jacob Goldstein

New York

Hachette Books
Hachette Book Group
1290 Avenue of the Americas
New York, NY 10104
HachetteBooks.com
Twitter.com/HachetteBooks
Instagram.com/HachetteBooks

First Trade Paperback Edition: October 2022

Published by Hachette Books, an imprint of Perseus Books, LLC, a subsidiary of
Hachette Book Group, Inc. The Hachette Books name and logo is a trademark of the
Hachette Book Group.

The Hachette Speakers Bureau provides a wide range of authors for speaking events.

To find out more, go to www.hachettespeakersbureau.com or call (866) 376-6591.

The publisher is not responsible for websites (or their content) that are not owned by
the publisher.

Library of Congress Cataloging-in-Publication Data has been applied for.

ISBNs: 978-0-316-41720-4 (trade paperback), 978-0-316-41719-8 (hardcover),
978-0-316-41718-1 (ebook), 978-0-306-92382-1 (int'l trade pbk.)

Printed in the United States of America

LSC-C

Printing 2, 2022

To Alexandra, Julia, and Olivia

Contents

III

More Money   75

IV

Modern Money   99

V

Twenty-First-Century Money   149

Money

Author's Note

Money Is Fiction

In the fall of 2008, I went out to dinner with my aunt Janet. She started life as a poet (the '60s) and wound up with an MBA (the '80s), so she's a good person to talk with about money. In the weeks before our dinner, trillions of dollars in wealth had suddenly vanished. I asked her where all that money went.

"Money is fiction," she said. "It was never there in the first place." That was the moment I realized money is weirder and more interesting than I thought.

I was working as a reporter at the *Wall Street Journal* at the time, but I covered health care and didn't know much about finance or economics. As the financial world fell apart, I started looking for anything that would explain what was going on. I discovered a podcast called *Planet Money*. The hosts didn't use dry, news-story language or voice-of-God anchorman tones. They talked like smart, funny people who were figuring out what was going on in the world and telling stories to explain it. I loved the show so much I went to work there.

By the time I got to *Planet Money*, the acute phase of the financial collapse was over, and we started looking at less urgent but more fundamental subjects. In 2011, we went on the radio show *This*

American Life to ask the question I'd been wrestling with since that dinner with my aunt: "What *is* money?"

The host, Ira Glass, called it "the most stoner question" he had ever posed on his show.

Maybe! But if so, it's the good kind of stoner question, the kind that still seems interesting in the sober light of morning. I returned to the idea of money again and again, chipping away little pieces, one episode at a time. Each little piece was interesting, but the more I learned, the more I felt like there was a deeper, richer story to tell. So I started working on this book.

Over time, I came to understand what my aunt meant when she said money is fiction. Money feels cold and mathematical and outside the realm of fuzzy human relationships. It isn't. Money is a made-up thing, a shared fiction. Money is fundamentally, unalterably social. The social part of money—the "shared" in "shared fiction"—is exactly what makes it money. Otherwise, it's just a chunk of metal, or a piece of paper, or, in the case of most money today, just a number stored on a bank's computers.

Like fiction, money has changed profoundly over time, and not in a steady or gentle way. When you look back, you see long periods of relative stability, and then suddenly, in some corner of the world, money goes bananas. Some wild genius has a new idea, or the world changes in some fundamental way that demands a new kind of money, or a financial collapse causes the monetary version of an existential crisis. The outcome is a profound change in the basic idea of money—what it is, who gets to create it, what it's supposed to do.

What counts as money (and what doesn't) is the result of choices we make, and those choices have a profound effect on who gets more stuff and who gets less, who gets to take risks when times are good, and who gets screwed when things go bad. Our choices about money gave us the world we live in now: the world where, when a pandemic hit in the spring of 2020, central banks could create trillions of dollars and euros and yen out of thin air in an effort to fight an economic collapse. In the future we'll make different choices, and money will change again.

These origin stories of money are the best way I know to understand what money is, and the power it has, and what we fight about when we fight about money. This book is the story of the moments—full of surprise and delight and brilliance and insanity—that gave us money as we know it today.

1

INVENTING MONEY

The origin of money isn't what we thought it was; the story is more messy and bloody and interesting. Marriage and murder are part of it. So is the invention of writing. Money and markets grow up together, and they make people more free but also, sometimes, more vulnerable.

CHAPTER 1

The Origin of Money

Around 1860, a French singer named Mademoiselle Zélie went on a world tour with her brother and two other singers. At a stop at a small island in the South Pacific, where most people didn't use money, the singers agreed to sell tickets in exchange for whatever goods the islanders could provide.

The show was a hit. A local chief attended. They sold 816 tickets. Zélie sang five songs from popular operas of the day. In a letter to her aunt, Zélie catalogued her pay for the show: "3 pigs, 23 turkeys, 44 hens, 5000 coconuts, 1200 pineapples, 120 bushels of bananas, 120 pumpkins, 1500 oranges." But the windfall, Zélie wrote, left her with a problem.

"What to do with these proceeds?"

If she were at the market in Paris, Zélie told her aunt, she could sell everything for 4,000 francs. A nice haul! "But here, how to resell this, how to cash in all this? The fact is that it is quite difficult to hope to find money from buyers who themselves have paid in pumpkins and coconuts for the pleasure of listening to us....

"I am told that a speculator from a nearby island...will arrive tomorrow to make cash offers to me and my comrades. In the meantime, to keep our pigs alive, we feed them the pumpkins while the turkeys and chickens eat the bananas and oranges."

In 1864, Zélie's letter was published as a footnote in a French book on the history of money. The British economist William Jevons loved the footnote so much that a decade later he used it to open his own book, *Money and the Mechanism of Exchange*. The moral of the story, for Jevons: barter sucks.

The trouble with barter, Jevons said, was that it required a "double coincidence" of wants. Not only did the islanders have to want what Mademoiselle Zélie offered (a concert); Zélie had to want what the islanders offered (pigs, chickens, coconuts). Human societies solved that problem, Jevons said, by agreeing on some relatively durable, relatively scarce thing to use as a token of value. We solved the problem of barter by inventing money.

Adam Smith had said the same thing a hundred years earlier, and Aristotle had said something similar a few thousand years before that. This theory—that money emerged from barter—is elegant and powerful and intuitive, but it suffers from one key weakness: there's no evidence that it's true. "No example of a barter economy, pure and simple, has ever been described, let alone the emergence from it of money," the anthropologist Caroline Humphrey wrote in 1985, summarizing what anthropologists and historians had been pointing out for decades.

The barter story reduces money to something cold and simple and objective: a tool for impersonal exchange. In fact, money is something much deeper and more complex.

People in pre-money societies were largely self-sufficient. They killed or grew or found their food, and they made their own stuff. There was some trade, but often it was part of formal rituals with strict norms of giving and getting. Money arose from these formal rituals at least as much as it did from barter.

In the case of Mademoiselle Zélie, the local custom where she visited would have been to take the pigs and turkeys and coconuts and bananas, and throw a feast for everybody. This would have given her status—like the status people get today for paying for a new hospital wing or university library. The guests at the feast would likely have been obliged in turn to throw a feast for Zélie. Entire economies were built on this kind of reciprocity.

On the northwest coast of North America, for example, at festivals called potlatch, Native American people spent days hanging out, making speeches, dancing, and giving stuff to each other. Gift giving was a power move, like insisting on paying the check at a restaurant. Before the Europeans arrived, high-status people gave furs and canoes. By the twentieth century, they were giving sewing machines and motorcycles. This wanton generosity freaked out the Canadians so much that the government made the practice illegal. People went to prison for giving stuff to each other.

Lots of cultures had precise rules about what you had to give somebody if you wanted to marry their child, or if you had killed their spouse. In many places, you had to give cattle; in other places it was cowrie shells. In Fiji it was sperm whales' teeth, and among Germanic tribes in Northern Europe it was rings made of gold, silver, or bronze. (Those tribes even had a specific word—*wergild*, "man payment"—for a payment to resolve a murder.) Rules for ritual sacrifice were often similarly explicit. In Vanuatu, a group of islands in the South Pacific, only certain pigs with especially big tusks could be sacrificed.

Once you know that anybody who is going to get married needs a string of cowrie shells, or that everybody who is going to attend the ritual sacrifice needs a long-tusked pig, you have an incentive to accumulate these things—even if you have no immediate need for them. Someone is going to need them soon enough. These objects become a way to store value over time. They are not quite money as we know it, but proto-money; they are money-adjacent. In Vanuatu, an elaborate web of borrowing and lending long-tusked pigs developed. Interest was based on the rate at which the tusks grew. An anthropologist reported that "a high proportion of the disputes and murders [were] over the payment or non-payment of pig debts."

Money isn't just some accounting device that makes exchange and saving more convenient. It's a deep part of the social fabric, bound up with blood and lust. No wonder we get so worked up over it.

IOU Six Sheep

Gift giving and reciprocity worked great in small villages built around family relationships, but they were a tough way to run a city. And by the time the first known cities began to emerge in Mesopotamia more than 5,000 years ago, people had started sealing little clay tokens inside hollow clay balls to represent debts. A little cone stood for a measure of barley; a disc stood for a sheep. If I gave you a ball with six discs inside, it meant IOU six sheep. At some point, people started pressing the tokens into the outside of the ball before sealing them in, to indicate what was inside. Eventually, somebody realized they didn't need to put the tokens inside the ball at all: they could just use the marking on the outside to represent the debt.

As Mesopotamian cities grew, power was centralized in urban temples and jobs became more specialized. Keeping track of who owed what to whom got more complicated. A class of people who worked for the temple (which functioned as a proto–city hall) figured out how to keep track of stuff by elaborating on the tokens-pressed-in-clay system. They used a reed stylus to make marks on a little clay tablet and started using abstract symbols for numbers themselves. The first writers weren't poets; they were accountants.

For a long time, that's all writing was. No love notes. No eulogies. No stories. Just IOU six sheep. Or, as a tablet from a famous mound in a Sumerian city called Uruk, in present-day Iraq, said: "Lu-Nanna, the head of the temple, received one cow and its two young suckling bull calves from the royal delivery from [a guy named] Abasaga."

Silver—a metal people had used previously for jewelry and rituals—was desirable and scarce and easy to store and divide, and it became money-ish in Mesopotamia, but for lots of people—maybe most people—money still wasn't a thing. They raised food and animals and ate what they grew. Once in a while, a tax collector who worked for the priest, or the queen, or the pharaoh, came around and took some of their barley and sheep. In some cities, the people who worked at the temple or palace also told the artisans who made cloth and bowls and jewelry what to make, and how much, then handed out the stuff as they saw fit.

The more some central authority decides who makes what and who gets what, the less a society needs money. In the Americas, thousands of years after the Mesopotamians, the Incas would create a giant, complex civilization without any money at all. The divine emperor (and the government bureaucrats who worked for him) told people what to grow, what to hunt, and what to make. Then the government took what they produced and redistributed it. Incan accountants kept detailed ledgers in the form of precisely knotted strings that recorded vast amounts of information. The Incas had rivers full of gold and mountains full of silver, and they used gold and silver for art and for worship. But they never invented money because it was a fiction they had no use for.

Money Changes Everything

For a long time, the kingdoms in ancient Greece ran largely on this kind of tribute and redistribution, complete with accountants who kept track of everything in their own specialized script. But that civilization collapsed around 1100 BC. Nobody knows why—maybe there was an earthquake, maybe there was a drought, maybe pirate raiders swept in. The kings disappeared, the castles fell down, the population declined, and the bureaucrats' accounting script was forgotten.

A few centuries later, the Greek population started growing again. Villages became towns. A class of artisans emerged. Trade led to specialization: fancy pottery in Athens, metalwork in Samos, roof tiles in Corinth. In 776 BC, Greeks converged for the first time on a town called Olympia for a month of sporting events; the birth of the Olympics was a sign of closer ties among Greek towns, and of Greeks getting rich enough to take a month off and go hang out in Olympia.

Greek towns started constructing public buildings and shared waterworks. It was the classic setting for an economy that revolved around a system of tribute and redistribution, controlled by a king or priest, which was still common in the civilizations to the east. But instead of creating top-down mini-kingdoms, the Greeks created something new. They called it the "polis," a word whose standard translation, "city-state," is so boring and generic that you could almost overlook the fact that the polis is the origin of much of political and economic life in the West. Not coincidentally, it was also the place where the first thing we would recognize today as money really took off.

Hundreds of poleis developed around the Greek world, and each had a citizen assembly. In some, including Athens, the polis evolved into democracy (though, by our standards, it was a crappy democracy that excluded women, slaves, and most immigrants). In other poleis, the assembly would meet and argue, but final decisions would be made by a smaller elite.

But in every case, the citizens—the polites—wanted a say in who gave what to whom. They needed a way to organize both public life and everyday exchange without a top-down, micromanaging ruler or a bottom-up web of kinship relations. They needed money!

Around 600 BC, Greece's neighbor Lydia, a kingdom in present-day Turkey, was mining a lot of a gold-silver alloy called electrum. This presented a kind of ancient first-world problem for the Lydians, because they had to assess the ratio of gold and silver in each piece to figure out its value. Somebody in Lydia came up with a clever solution: they started taking lumps of electrum with a consistent ratio of gold to silver, breaking them into standard sizes, and stamping the image of a lion onto each lump. So every lump of a given size had the same value as every other lump of that size. The Lydians had invented coins. Soon, they took the next step: they started minting coins of pure silver and pure gold.

Greece might have flourished if coins didn't exist. Coins probably would have spread even if Greece didn't exist (for the story of coins in China, see the next chapter). But coins and Greece were a perfect match, and the Greeks went wild for coins.

Standardized lumps of metal were exactly what the city-states needed to build their new kind of society—a society too big to run on familial reciprocity but too egalitarian to run on tribute—and soon there were a hundred different mints spread across Greece making silver coins. Within a few more decades, the money-ish things the Greeks had been using to measure value and exchange goods (iron cooking spits, lumps of silver) weren't money-ish anymore. Money was coins, and coins were money.

Coins transformed daily life in Greece. Each Greek city-state had a public space called the agora where citizens gathered to hear speeches and talk about the news and in some cases have formal meetings of the citizens. Around the time coins arrived, people started showing up at the agora with stuff to sell. Soon the agora became the market—this new kind of place where ordinary people went to buy and sell cloth and figs and pots and everything else. The agora also continued to be a place for public discussion, but in the long run shopping won out over public discourse. In modern Greek, the word *agora* is a noun that means market, and a verb that means to buy.

Before the arrival of coins, poor Greeks would work on the farms of rich landowners, but they didn't get anything like a wage as we would understand it. They would agree to work for a season or a year, and the landowner would agree to give them food and clothes and a place to sleep. In the decades after coins arrived, that changed. Poor people became day laborers, showing up in the morning and getting paid at the end of the day. The practice of signing on to work for a year at a time vanished. Poor workers no longer had to stay on a farm for a year; they could leave if they were badly treated or if they found a better arrangement. But no one was responsible anymore for feeding them and clothing them and giving them a place to stay. They were on their own.

People flowed into the new wage-based economy. Women sold ribbons and picked grapes, though it was considered a sign of desperation when a citizen's wife had to work for money. When the Athenians built a new temple on the Acropolis in the fifth century, slaves did a lot of the work, but wage laborers did some of the detail finishes, like carving the fluting into the columns at the front of the temple. Because a random accounting tablet happened to survive, we know that the slaves worked almost every day, but the wage laborers worked less than two-thirds of the time. Were the laborers choosing to take time off because they preferred to do something else? Or were they denied work that they needed to survive? As the scholar David Schaps asked, was it "the blessing of leisure or the curse of unemployment"?

The spread of coins—the rise of money—made people more free and gave them more opportunities to leave the life they'd been born into. It also made people more isolated and vulnerable.

Not everybody liked what coins were doing to Greece. Aristotle complained about Greeks who thought of wealth as "only a quantity of coin," and called getting rich in retail trade "unnatural." Complaints like these would follow money forever, but they didn't matter much in the end. Once coins took root in Greece, they took over the world.

CHAPTER 2

When We Invented Paper Money, Had an Economic Revolution, Then Tried to Forget the Whole Thing Ever Happened

In 1271, Marco Polo went to Asia. Twenty-five years later, he went home to Venice, bought a ship to fight in a war against Genoa, got captured and thrown in jail, and dictated a book about his travels to his cellmate, a Pisan who was a writer of popular books, including the first Italian version of the story of King Arthur. Marco Polo's book is important for lots of reasons, but for our purposes it's huge because of chapter 24, which has the long-but-worth-it title: *How the Great Kaan Causeth the Bark of Trees, Made into Something Like Paper, to Pass for Money Over All His Country.*

Polo starts the chapter by saying: This is so crazy, you're not going to believe me. ("For, tell it how I might, you never would be satisfied that I was keeping within truth and reason.") He was right. His story about paper passing as money seemed so absurd to people in Europe that they thought he was making it up. (To be fair, they thought he was making a lot of stuff up, and some stuff he did make up, but we know now that what Marco Polo said about money was true.) He saw in China a radical monetary experiment that appeared in the world for a moment, then disappeared and wouldn't return anywhere on Earth for hundreds of years. What Polo saw reveals the fundamental economic miracle of an entire society starting to rise out of poverty—and how fleeting that miracle can be.

For a long time before the age of Marco Polo (really, for all of the time before the age of Marco Polo), interaction between China and Europe was pretty limited. The Chinese invented coins around the same time the Lydians did, possibly earlier, but as far as anybody knows that was just a coincidence.

Some of the earliest Chinese coins were tiny knives and tiny shovels made out of bronze, which may have been a vestige of real knives and shovels serving as money-adjacent stuff. Eventually, coins turned into small pieces of bronze with a hole through the middle. The hole let people string a bunch of coins together to make it easier to carry them. This was useful because the value of coins was based on the value of metal they contained, and bronze wasn't very valuable, so it took lots of bronze coins to buy stuff. The standard unit became a string of 1,000 coins, which weighed more than seven pounds.

By the early part of the first century AD, China had become a unified, bureaucratic empire. Tens of thousands of students took competitive exams to get high-status government jobs, and the lucky few who managed to land those jobs spent their working lives keeping extensive records written on silk and on tablets made of wood or bamboo. Treaties were written in triplicate: one copy for each side in the dispute, and a third for the spirits.

As record keeping proliferated, the expense of silk and the

bulkiness of wood and bamboo became a problem: Chinese officials needed something better suited for all that paperwork. They needed paper. According to official records, they got it in 105 AD, when a eunuch named Cai Lun, the emperor's "officer in charge of tools and weapons," ground up mulberry bark, rags, and fish nets; dipped a screen into the mash; then let the mash dry on the screen. People loved paper, and Cai became rich and famous. (For a while, anyway. Eventually, Cai was accused of falsifying some financial paperwork, so he took a bath, put on his fanciest clothes, drank poison, and died.)

Printing came a few hundred years later, driven in part by the spread of Buddhism, which prized reproducing sacred texts. Some monk who was tired of writing the same sacred text over and over and over had the truly brilliant idea of transferring the text to a wood block, carving away everything that was not the sacred text, then covering the block with ink and stamping it onto paper. The earliest surviving printed text is a paper scroll with a Buddhist prayer printed in China around 710 AD.

Now China had paper, and printing, and coins. The final step came two centuries later in the province of Sichuan. Most Chinese coins were made of bronze, but in Sichuan, where bronze was scarce, they used iron. In a world where the value of a coin was based largely on the value of the metal it was made of, iron was a terrible thing to use for money. To buy a pound of salt, you needed a pound and a half of iron coins. It would be like having to do all your shopping using only pennies.

Around 995 AD, a merchant in Sichuan's capital, Chengdu, had an idea. He started letting people leave their iron coins with him. In exchange for coins, he would give people fancy, standardized paper receipts. The receipts were like coat-check tickets for coins. And just like anyone with a coat-check ticket can claim the coat, anyone with a receipt could claim the coins: the receipts were transferable. Pretty soon, rather than go to the trouble of getting their coins every time they wanted to make a purchase, people started using the coat-check receipts to buy stuff: the paper itself turned into money. (The merchant didn't invent this out of thin air. Provincial governments had previously given traders paper receipts in exchange for bronze coins, but traders typically just used those receipts to avoid taking coins on long journeys; those receipts never really took off as money.)

Other merchants started issuing their own paper receipts. Inevitably, some shady merchant figured out that he didn't need to start with a deposit of iron coins. He could just print up an IOU, go out in the world, and buy something with it. Once that happened, it was only a matter of time before someone came to trade in that IOU for iron coins and found out it was just a worthless piece of paper. People got angry. There were lawsuits. After a few years, the government took over the business of printing paper money.

For people who couldn't read, most bills had a handy picture of the number of coins they could be exchanged for. There was usually some kind of landscape or streetscape. The bills were printed in multiple colors—text in black, landscape in blue, official seal in red. Almost always, a big chunk of the bill was taken up by a warning like this one, from a bill printed around 1100 AD:

> By imperial decree: criminals who counterfeit [this bill] are to be punished by beheading. The reward [for informers] shall be 1,000 guan.... If accomplices of counterfeiters or any who harbor them willingly identify the ringleaders to the authorities they will be absolved of criminal liability and given the above-stipulated reward.

The warning wasn't entirely successful: The earliest surviving printing plates for paper money are counterfeits. But despite the forgeries, paper money was a hit.

At a time when transporting large quantities of heavy coins made trade difficult or impossible, paper money was a breakthrough. As it spread across China, trade increased, people learned more from each other, and technology improved. Paper money even changed how people worked. For hundreds of years, taxes had been collected in cloth and grain, forcing people to weave and plant simply to meet the government's demands. Now the government shifted toward collecting taxes in coins and paper. Suddenly, people were free (or freer, anyway) to choose what to do.

✳ ✳ ✳

Scholars describe an "economic revolution" at this moment in China, hundreds of years before Europe's own industrial revolution. Movable type and the magnetic compass were invented. Farmers figured out new agricultural techniques that allowed them to grow far more rice in the same amount of space. Printed books spread information on these breakthroughs around the country. More and more people moved out of a feudal(-ish) economy that ran on tribute, and into a market economy that ran on money. Now people could specialize in what they and their land were best suited for. Some grew mulberry trees, the leaves of which were fed to silkworms to make silk, and the bark of which was mashed into paper. Some grew seeds that were pressed into oils for "cooking, lighting, waterproofing, and to go in hair creams and medicines." Some farmers started fish hatcheries; others built special containers to transport baby fish hundreds of miles to ponds best suited for raising the fish to maturity.

Earlier emperors had confined markets to small, government-supervised blocks where prices were rigidly controlled. Merchants who tried to sell outside these markets were buried alive, a hundred at a time. Now, rules on markets were loosened, and people could sell what they wanted, where they wanted.

Markets and money made cities. At a time when fewer than 100,000 people lived in London and Paris, two Chinese cities grew to more than a million people each. In Hangzhou, China's southern capital, a restaurant scene appeared. Money now bought meals at cheap noodle shops, spicy Szechuan places, and fancy restaurants known for specialties like goose with apricots and noodles stuffed with pork. One account from the time suggests hip, urban diners were as insufferable then as they are now:

> As soon as the customers have chosen where they will sit, they are asked what they want to have. The people...are very difficult to please. Hundreds of orders are given on all sides: this person wants something hot, another something cold, a third something tepid, a fourth something chilled; one wants cooked food, another raw, another chooses roast, another grill....

The normal state of human affairs for most of human history was economic stasis: people, on average, did not become richer over time. In China, around the time paper money emerged, that changed. The money-driven growth of markets went hand in hand with technological breakthroughs, and as a result, a day's work started to buy more stuff than it used to. People—not just a few people, but lots of people—were getting richer. This is the fundamental economic miracle, and it is the only way to sustainably raise the standard of living over the long run. (Not coincidentally, intensive growth may also have emerged in ancient Greece around the time coins were invented, but it didn't last.) By 1200, China was quite possibly the richest and certainly the most technologically advanced civilization in the world.

Then the Mongols rode in.

Money Backed by Nothing

In 1215, Genghis Khan's army captured what is now Beijing. Forty-five years later, his grandson Kublai was elected Great Khan, and took control of the biggest empire in the world.

The vast reach of the Mongol empire was great for trade. Now the market for Chinese goods extended not just throughout China, but across Asia and beyond. In cottage factories, Chinese artisans carved images of the Madonna and Child for export to Europe. An especially smooth type of Chinese silk also became popular in Europe. Shiploads of the stuff left from a Chinese port that Arab traders called Zaytun, which sounded to British ears like "satin," so that's what they called the fabric that came from there. The famous Moroccan scholar and traveler Ibn Battuta described Chinese trading ships that had four decks and carried a thousand people.

The Mongols were nomads, and they loved how much easier it was to move paper money than metal coins. They understood that speed meant wealth. So the year Kublai became the Great Khan, he created a new kind of paper money, to be used across vast swaths of the empire. He called it the "inaugural treasure exchange voucher." (It's not just paper; it's a voucher you can exchange for treasure!) Kublai Khan really wanted people to use his new paper money, so he made it illegal to use bronze coins for trade. And as

Marco Polo saw when he arrived a few years later, the Great Khan's plan worked.

> This paper money is circulated in every part of the Great Khan's dominions; nor dares any person, at the peril of his life, refuse to accept it in payment. All of his subjects receive it without hesitation, because, wherever their business may call them, they can dispose of it again in the purchase of merchandise they may require; such as pearls, jewels, gold, or silver. With it, in short, every article may be procured....All of his Majesty's armies are paid with this currency, which is to them of the same value as if it were gold or silver. Upon these grounds, it may certainly be affirmed that the Great Khan has a more extensive command of treasure than any other sovereign in the universe.

Being able to literally print money is awesome (it's good to be the Khan), but with great power comes a great desire to print more and more. Kublai Khan resisted for a while, but eventually the temptation was too strong to bear. After all, Japan was sitting right there, across a little sea, just begging to be invaded. Why not print up a little more paper so we can pay people to build ships to sail 70,000 soldiers and horses over there to show them who's universal sovereign?

In 1287, after not one but two failed invasions of Japan, Kublai Khan issued a new kind of paper money. The paper still had pictures of bronze coins on it, but this time they were just pictures. Government offices refused to redeem the paper for silver or bronze; people could no longer exchange their treasure exchange vouchers for treasure. We have to imagine there was some panic. There was inflation: prices rose as money became less valuable. But then the economy stabilized. The center held. Pieces of paper that were just paper, that weren't even pretending to be treasure vouchers or silver IOUs, still worked as money.

This is the radical experiment that Marco Polo witnessed: money as almost pure abstraction, backed by nothing. It would be like if Wile E. Coyote ran off the cliff, looked down, saw empty space below him—and didn't fall. Partly this is a testament to the sheer power of the Mongol state: use this paper as money or I'll kill you. But partly, after three hundred years of using paper money, people in China had figured out that paper money worked not because it was backed by silver or bronze, but because everybody agreed paper could be money.

* * *

The era we live in now bears a bit of resemblance to China 1,000 years ago. Because of technological change, most people are richer than their ancestors were. This started in England about 250 years ago, with the industrial revolution. One of the oldest questions in economic history is: Why then and there? After thousands of years of economic and technological muddling along, what changed in England around 1800? Some people cite intellectual and legal changes like the scientific revolution and clearly defined property rights. Others take a more practical approach, arguing that the relatively high wages of British workers inspired people to create labor-saving machines, and that Britain just happened to have vast quantities of coal on hand to power those machines.

But in the past few decades, as Western economists have become less Eurocentric, they've noticed that technological improvements and economic growth didn't start two hundred years ago in England. China had its own economic revolution eight hundred years before England's. And while economic growth didn't explode in China the way it would in Europe, Chinese inventions from that era—paper, printing, the magnetic compass—were essential for Europe's development. Now, scholars are asking a new question: What happened to China? It was on the cutting edge of economic sophistication and new technology in 1300, but far behind by 1900. Why?

Maybe it's because China, as the dominant state in the region, wasn't constantly pushing to economically outcompete its neighbors, so it stagnated relative to the European states that were always at war with each other. Maybe it's because labor in China was cheap, so there was little incentive to continually invent labor-saving devices. Another reason is particularly compelling for our story: the Chinese rebel leader who drove out the Mongols really didn't like money or markets.

The man who became known as the Hongwu emperor was the child of poor farmers who died by the time he was sixteen. He entered a Buddhist monastery to avoid starving to death, then joined a band of anti-Mongol rebels and fought his way up through the ranks. In 1368, after the Mongols were pushed north of the Great Wall, Hongwu founded the Ming Dynasty, which would last for nearly three hundred years.

Hongwu wanted to take China back to a (totally idealized) past, a time not just before the Mongol invasion, but before China's economic revolution. He dreamed of a nation of self-sufficient agricultural villages where people grew and shared what they needed. So he and his successors systematically got rid of the economic changes that drove China's economic revolution. They banned overseas trading. They moved away from a money-and-markets economy back toward an ancient system of tribute and redistribution, in which the government took cloth and grain from peasants and gave it to government workers.

By the mid-1400s, paper money had disappeared from China

entirely. People used lumps of silver as money, and sometimes copper coins, and often no money at all. The emperor had succeeded in dragging China back to the past. The average person in China was poorer than her ancestors had been two hundred years earlier. The economic revolution that happened when paper money was invented was largely forgotten.

Because it happened a thousand years ago, China's golden economic age of technological breakthroughs and paper money and fancy restaurants feels like a blip. And on a very long time horizon, it was dwarfed by the technological and economic growth of the past few centuries.

But there's another way of looking at this blip: It lasted about as long as our current experiment with paper money and technological breakthroughs and fancy restaurants has lasted so far.

Today, we take economic growth and scientific discoveries for granted. If the economy shrinks even a little bit, for a few seasons in a row, we declare it a recession and wonder what the problem is and when it will get better. But one thing China's three-hundred-year-blip tells us is this: economic growth and technological change aren't guaranteed to continue forever. Development is not a one-way street. Civilizations don't just get richer or stay the same. Sometimes they become poorer, generation after generation. Sometimes money itself disappears.

11

THE MURDERER,
THE BOY KING, AND
THE INVENTION OF
CAPITALISM

*In Europe in the 1600s, a bunch of things started happening at once.
Goldsmiths accidentally became bankers. A tiny country invented the
stock market and the modern corporation and became fabulously rich.
And gamblers discovered a fundamentally new way of thinking about
money and the future. These threads came together to create modern
capitalism.*

The hero/anti-hero of the era is John Law. He starts out sticking his head into the corner of a few early frames as this new world is emerging. By the end of the era Law is at the center of everything. He creates a modern economy for an entire nation, becomes the richest non-king in the world, and seizes control of nearly half of what is now the continental United States—but only after being convicted of murder, going on the lam for twenty years, and winning a fortune as a gambler. The world Law was born into, and the world he created, explain a lot about how money, banks, and, really, entire nations still succeed and fail.

CHAPTER 3

How Goldsmiths Accidentally Re-Invented Banks (and Brought Panic to Britain)

In seventeenth-century England, money was a mess.

Ever since coins were invented, people had tried to steal a little metal out of them by clipping them along the edges or by putting them in a bag and shaking them to get a little silver or gold dust to fall off. Responsible governments would regularly mint new coins (the way modern governments replace torn bills with new ones) to freshen up the supply.

England in the 1600s did not have a responsible government, and by the second half of the century, it was common for silver coins to contain much less silver than they were supposed to. Every time somebody had to pay somebody else, buyer and seller had to decide: Is this coin worth what it's supposed to be worth, or is it worth less because there's not enough silver in it?

Workers and employers argued over pay. Fistfights broke out at markets. "Nothing could be purchased without a dispute," the historian Thomas Macaulay wrote later. "Over every counter there was a wrangling from morning to night." Contracts started to stipulate not just how much money was to be paid, but the total weight of the coins in a payment. History ran in reverse. Coins became less like money and more like lumps of precious metal.

A second problem made things even worse. Because of international price differences, people could profit by taking full-weight silver coins out of England and trading them for gold in Paris or Amsterdam. As a result, even when the British mint did make good new silver coins, people almost immediately took those coins out of circulation to go trade them for gold in another country.

So the British never had enough silver coins, and the silver coins they did have were terrible coins that nobody trusted. England needed more money. Not more wealth, just more tokens so people could buy and sell stuff.

Then, without really meaning to, goldsmiths started to solve the not-enough-money problem. Also without really meaning to, they created a new kind of problem that's still with us today.

Rich people sometimes stored their gold and silver in the vaults of local goldsmiths. Goldsmiths gave people receipts—just like that merchant in Sichuan had done hundreds of years earlier. In time, people started using the receipts themselves to buy and sell stuff. But this was just a substitution of paper for metal; it wasn't adding more money to the world. The next step was the big one, the leap that not only links seventeenth-century goldsmiths with modern banks, but also explains why modern banks are both so essential and so dangerous.

Goldsmiths started giving people loans. No longer did you have to actually give the goldsmith your gold to get a claim check. You could just give him a promise to pay him back, with interest. In exchange for your promise, he would give you some of those claim checks that were circulating as money. Then you could walk out into the streets of London and use the paper to start buying stuff. Suddenly, there was more money circulating in London than there used to be—the goldsmith had created money out of thin air. The goldsmiths were solving the not-enough-money problem.

Right around the same time, something similar happened in Sweden, where people were especially eager to try paper money. The Swedes had a lot of copper, and they used copper for their coins. Copper wasn't very valuable, so the coins were very big. Coin isn't even really the right word: the largest denomination of Swedish money, worth 10 dalers, was two feet long and weighed forty-three pounds. People carried them strapped to their backs. So the Swedes created a bank that gave people paper money in exchange for giant copper coins. Like the goldsmiths in England, the Swedish bank almost immediately also started giving people paper money as loans. It was just so hard to resist; the paper money was just sitting there.

Banks today do what the British goldsmiths did almost four hundred years ago: when you deposit money, the bank turns around and lends some of it out to someone else. That money—your money—is now in two places at once. It is your money, in your account at the bank. It is also the borrower's money. The borrower can deposit her money at another bank, which can then lend some of it out to yet another borrower. The same dollar is now in three places at once. This is called fractional-reserve banking, and it's how the vast majority of money in the world is created.

This feels spooky, and for good reason. Even as the goldsmiths were transforming British banking forever and starting to solve the not-enough-money problem, they were creating a new problem. The goldsmiths were giving out more gold claim checks than they had gold. If everybody with a claim check came back at the same time and demanded their gold, the goldsmiths (and the people who wanted their gold back) would be screwed. Today, when everybody with money in the bank comes and asks for it at the same time, we call it a bank run. And the banks and the people who want their money back—which is to say, basically, everybody—are still screwed.

While paper money was new to Europe, banking and bank runs were not. In Venice, money changers had started storing gold for people in the fourteenth century—and lending that gold out to other people. The money changers sat on benches on a busy bridge over the Grand Canal, so they were called *banchieri*, which translates as "bench-sitters," and which is the root of our words *banker* and *bank*. To reduce the risk of bank runs, the Venetians required the bench-sitters to keep a certain percentage of gold in reserve. Barcelona had a more aggressive regulatory regime: bankers who couldn't pay back depositors had to live on bread and water, and in 1360 one bankrupt Barcelona banker was beheaded in front of his bench.

Bank runs came to London right after the goldsmiths turned into bankers. The goldsmiths had loaned a lot of gold to King Charles, and in 1672, Charles needed money to wage war against the Dutch, so he decided to stop paying the goldsmiths back. (It's good to be the king.) People in London looked at those pieces of paper the goldsmiths had given them—the claim checks—and got nervous. Everybody went to their goldsmiths and asked for the gold back, and, of course, there wasn't enough gold. Some goldsmiths went bankrupt. A few were imprisoned for debt. At least one fled the country. Suddenly, those goldsmith notes didn't seem so much like money anymore. Just two weeks after the king stopped paying his bills, the treasurer of the navy worried that he had "taken notes which is now not money."

The thing that makes money *money* is trust—when we trust that we will be able to buy stuff with this piece of paper, or this lump of metal, tomorrow, and next month, and next year. One of the perpetual questions that still hovers over money is: Who can we trust? The British had tried trusting the government, but government-minted coins weren't doing the job. So they turned to goldsmiths, and that didn't work out so well. It would take another generation before they finally found something that worked: a solution that was neither purely private nor purely public, but a combination of the two, with the interests of the government and the interests of bankers and the interests of the people all pushing against each other.

John Law's First Act

John Law was born, almost too perfectly, upstairs from a goldsmith's shop in Edinburgh. The goldsmith was his father, and the year was 1671, just before the run on the goldsmith bankers in London.

As John grew up, his dad grew rich. When John was twelve, his father bought a little castle outside of Edinburgh. Around the same time, Law went off to boarding school, where he excelled in math and a subject called "manly pursuits," which, somewhat disappointingly, mostly means he was good at tennis.

Law finished school, moved to London, chased women, bought clothes he couldn't afford, and started gambling all the time. He was known in the parlance of the time as a beau, which rhymes with bro, and is kind of similar but more highbrow. Law's father died, and John gambled away his inheritance and had to sell the castle to pay his debts. In classic bro fashion, he was bailed out by his mom, who had her own inheritance, and bought the castle from him to keep it in the family and to keep Law out of debtors' prison.

In the spring of the next year—on April 9, 1694, just as he was turning twenty-three—John Law had an encounter that would lead (indirectly, but still) to one of the biggest, wildest experiments in the history of money.

Law was standing in Bloomsbury Square, on the outskirts of London, in the middle of the day, as a carriage rolled up. A young man got out, walked up to Law, and drew his sword. Law drew his own sword and struck the other man. The other man fell down and died.

The other man was Edward Wilson, who, like Law, was a young London beau. The encounter was a duel, planned in advance to resolve a dispute. Nobody knows what the fight was about, but, like most fights, it probably had something to do with money or love or honor.

Wilson was the fifth son of a middling, indebted aristocrat, yet he lived like the richest man in London. No one knew where all his money came from. Some people gossiped at the time that the king's mistress fell in love with Wilson and funneled him royal money. Thirty years later, an anonymous pamphlet appeared suggesting another story: "Love-Letters Between a Certain Late Nobleman and the Famous Mr. Wilson: Discovering the True History of the Rise and Surprising Grandeur of that Celebrated Beau." Maybe a certain late nobleman had been giving Wilson hush money. One of Law's most recent and most thorough biographers, the economist Antoin Murphy, suggests that someone—the king or the nobleman—wanted to keep Wilson from telling his secrets, and somehow persuaded Law to kill Wilson.

Law was living with a woman who was married to another man. Wilson's sister for a while was living in the same building as Law, then left in a huff, offended by the sin going on under her roof. Wilson found out about it and confronted Law. According to one version of the story, that is what led to the duel.

Whatever the cause of the fight, the crime was clear. Dueling was illegal in seventeenth century England, and Law was arrested, thrown in jail, and convicted of the murder of Edward Wilson. He was sentenced to death by hanging. (Four other people were sentenced to be hanged at the same time. Two of them were sentenced for creating counterfeit coins, and one was sentenced for trimming silver off existing coins. As in medieval China, the British government killed people to try to keep the money sound.)

Law didn't expect to be killed. Dueling was relatively common among gentlemen, and no one could remember anybody being put to death for it. Initially, it looked like the king would pardon him. But Wilson's family fought against a pardon. The king wavered; Law languished.

Then, in the first week of 1695, Law escaped from the King's Bench Prison. The details are unclear, but from letters written at the time it appears that Law had powerful friends who got the warden to look the other way while an accomplice drugged the guards and opened the door of Law's cell. Law, now a fugitive, got on a boat to Europe.

He was about to discover an intellectual revolution that was changing the way people thought about the future and about money. Law would use that revolution to get rich.

CHAPTER 4

How to Get Rich with Probability

The next ten years of Law's life are obscure. He disappears from the historical record, then pops up in Paris, and in Venice, and in Amsterdam. Every time he emerges from the mist, he is gambling with local elites. And every time, he wins. It's not that he was lucky. It doesn't seem like he cheated. Law won because he discovered an intellectual discipline—a way of looking at the world—that was emerging during his lifetime and that would eventually shape the way millions of people thought about God, money, death, and the unknown future. The discipline is probability theory. It's the basis of much of modern finance and, for that matter, much of modern thought. It was invented by gamblers.

People had been gambling forever; four-sided knucklebones used as dice have been found in ancient archaeological sites around the world. But, almost unbelievably to our modern sensibility, gamblers had never really done the math. They knew that some outcomes were more likely than others. But they knew it in a fuzzy, quali- tative way. Now, finally, gamblers started to calculate exactly how likely they were to win or lose. At a time when most people still thought of outcomes as luck or divine providence, doing the math at the gambling table was like having a superpower.

One of the most important of the gambler-mathematicians was the weirdo genius Blaise Pascal. As a teenager, he had written a treatise on geometry that was good enough to impress Descartes (who was in the midst of inventing a branch of modern geometry). He invented a mechanical calculator, which he named after himself (the Pascaline), which never took off, possibly because it was too expensive to produce. For a while, when he was in his twenties, Pascal had a religious crisis and gave up gambling. "Who has placed me here?" he wrote. "By whose order and warrant was this place and this time ordained for me? The eternal silence of these infinite spaces leaves me in terror." When he was twenty-seven, these intense questions caused a sort of physical breakdown—headaches, difficulty swallowing—so he turned his back on the existential abyss and walked back to the gambling tables.

In 1654, a French mathematician and gambler called the Chevalier de Méré asked Pascal a couple of questions. One was about the probability of rolling double sixes given several chances. The other was a deeper, more complicated question that gamblers had been puzzling over for more than a century.

It was known as the "problem of the points," and it went like this. Two players put money in the pot and agree that whoever wins a certain number of rounds of a game will take the pot. It can be any game of chance—dice rolls, coin flips, whatever. The players start the game, but they have to stop before they've completed the agreed number of rounds. What's a fair system for splitting the pot based on the score when the game is stopped?

These questions inspired Pascal to write to Pierre de Fermat, a lawyer who moonlighted as a math genius. They sent letters back and forth for a few months, working on the problems. The problem of rolling double sixes was easy. The problem of the points took a little longer—and the solution Pascal and Fermat worked out had a more profound impact on the history of money, and of human thought.

Here's a simple example of the problem. Say you and I each put £50 into the pot, and agree that all £100 will go to whoever wins a best-of-three series of coin flips. You bet on heads, I bet on tails. You flip once; it comes up heads. Then we have to stop the game before we have time to flip again. You're up one to zero. How should we split the £100?

Pascal and Fermat's insight was to consider every possible outcome of the game, and then figure out what percentage of the outcomes each player would win and split the pot accordingly. They worked out the math in detail, but we can look at the simple example below without getting into much math.

If we stop a best-of-three bet after a single flip, when you have one heads and I have zero tails, here are the possible outcomes of the two remaining flips:

1. heads, heads (you win)

2. tails, heads (you win)

3. heads, tails (you win)

4. tails, tails (I win)

You win 75 percent of the time (three out of four), and I win 25 percent of the time (one out of four). Of the £100 in the pot, you should get £75 and I should get £25.

What is maybe most surprising about this solution is how unsurprising it seems to us. So obvious! What is so extraordinary—the whole point of the story—is that, in thousands of years of gambling, as far as we know, nobody had figured it out before, because people did not think about the uncertain future as something you could calculate. The future was determined by chance, or the gods, or God; it was not determined by math. That's why this was such a transformative moment in the history of thought, and of money. It's why a Stanford mathematician recently wrote an entire book about Pascal and Fermat's solution to this problem: "It set out, for the first time, a method whereby humans can predict the future."

A few years after his correspondence with Fermat, Pascal went back to the edge of the existential abyss. But he brought this new kind of thinking with him. "God is, or He is not," Pascal wrote. "But to which side shall we incline? Reason can decide nothing here....A game is being played at the extremity of this infinite distance where heads or tails will turn up. What will you wager?"

If you wager that "God is" (for Pascal, this meant the Christian God), and you win, what you get is "an eternity of life and happiness." If you bet that "God is not," and you win, you get to be right. It's a bet where the payoff for one side is infinitely larger than the payoff for the other side—an eternity of life and happiness versus being right. The choice is obvious. "Wager, then, without hesitation that He is."

Pascal made that bet. His mathematical thinking inspired him to give up math, sell almost everything he owned, and move into a monastery. Probabilistic thinking had jumped the species barrier. Now it wasn't just about dice and money; it was about everything.

Probability in the Wild

The ideas of Pascal and Fermat spread quickly among Europe's intellectuals. A few decades later, their ideas reached John Law (this was presumably after he nearly lost the family castle at the gambling table). "No man understood calculation and numbers better than he," one of Law's friends wrote. "He was the first man in England that was at pains to find out...all the other chances of the dice."

Law would hand a player a six-sided die and offer 10,000-to-1 odds against rolling six sixes in a row. He knew that the odds of doing so were roughly 1 in 50,000 (or 1 in 6^6). When he was on the lam in Paris in the early 1700s, he arrived at the gambling tables with bags full of gold. He would often play the role of the house, or the banker, in games where the odds slightly favored the house. He kept winning. His bets eventually grew so large that he had his own gold chips minted.

As Law was using probability to get rich, his contemporaries were using it to change the way people thought about death (and money). Up until this time, people thought about death sort of like they thought about dice: they knew it was more likely for some people (babies, old people) than for others (teenagers). But they didn't know it by the numbers. They were like gamblers before probability theory: they didn't do the math.

This turned out to be a big problem for European governments, which raised money at the time not by collecting regular income taxes, but by selling annuities (among other schemes). To buy an annuity, I pay the government a lump sum (say, £1,000) and in exchange the government promises me a fixed annual payment (say, £70) for the rest of my life.

An annuity is, awkwardly, a bet on how long the buyer will live. If I buy an annuity today, and I die tomorrow, the government gets to keep all my money and doesn't have to pay me anything. I lose, and the government wins. If I live to one hundred, the government has to send me those sweet, sweet annuity checks every year for decades. The government loses, and I win. In John Law's day, governments and their citizens were making these bets, but nobody knew how long people were likely to live. They were playing dice, but they didn't know the odds.

In England at the time, an annuity was the same price no matter the age of the person who bought it. So everybody started buying annuities for their teenage kids, who were likely to live a long time and make a huge profit. Good for the kids, bad for England.

The British mathematician Edmond Halley knew of the work of Pascal and Fermat and figured the math for annuities should be solvable. By the time he was thirty-three years old, Halley had already traveled halfway around the world to map the stars, and helped his pal Isaac Newton publish *The Principia*, the book that laid out the theory of gravity. (Predicting the return of an as-yet-unnamed comet was still a few years off for Halley.) Around this time, he became editor of this new kind of thing, a scientific journal, and he had the same problem that every editor of every publication has had for all of history: he had to find stuff to fill up his pages. So when he heard about this Eastern European town called Breslaw, where they kept unusually good records of citizens' births and deaths, he had an idea.

In January 1693, Halley published "An Estimate of the Degrees of the Mortality of Mankind, drawn from curious Tables of the Births and Funerals at the City of Breslaw; with an Attempt to ascertain the Price of Annuities upon Lives."

In the very first sentence he ran straight at the heart of his subject with the all promiscuous capitalization of the era: "The contemplation of the Mortality of Mankind, has besides the Moral, its Physical and Political Uses...." *Yes, I know, death is bound up with everything deep about being human, but also it's a physical thing in the world and we need to understand what it means for us as a nation.* Halley shouted out the few other people who had recently tried to analyze the mortality rate for citizens of London and Dublin, but he pointed out that none of them had access to all the information they needed, because nobody in London or Dublin was keeping close enough track of births and deaths. Now, these records from Breslaw had appeared.

Then Halley started doing lots of math. And after complaining about the "most laborious calculation," he figured out exactly how likely people of different ages were to die. Someone who just turned twenty had a 1 percent chance of dying before her next birthday. A fifty-year-old had a 3 percent chance of dying before age fifty-one. "A man of 30 may reasonably expect to live between 27 and 28 years," he wrote. And so on.

Halley thought an annuity would be fairly priced if the buyer who lived exactly as long as the average person got paid back exactly as much as she put in. If she died early, she'd collect less than she put in; if she lived longer, she'd collect more. And he saw clearly that England was selling its annuities too cheaply: everybody under age sixty was likely to get more back than they put in.

This wasn't just some random set of morbid facts or a useful piece of accounting. It was a method. Given the data of births and deaths for a given population, anybody could now figure out how likely people were to die at any age. Halley had solved the problem of the points, but for life itself.

A few decades later, a pair of hard-drinking Scottish ministers named Alexander Webster and Robert Wallace thought Halley's tables from a random town in Central Europe might help them with a problem they were trying to solve: how to provide for the wives and children of Scottish ministers who died young.

Life insurance was already a thing but, as with annuities before Halley came along, nobody really knew the odds. Like annuities, life insurance is a bet on how long the insured will live, but the winners and losers are reversed. As a buyer, I win ("win") if I buy a policy and then die right away, so my family gets a big payout when I've only paid in a little bit. But of course it only works if the life insurance company has the money to pay. If the company runs out of money because it's been selling policies too cheaply, my family is out of luck.

To launch the Scottish Ministers' Widows' Fund, Wallace and Webster used Halley's tables, and the new science of probability, and the help of a mathematician friend, to estimate how much each minister had to chip in. Wallace and Webster predicted there would be £47,401 in the fund ten years after it launched. The prediction was phenomenally accurate: the real figure turned out to be £47,313. They were off by less than 1 percent. An intellectual revolution made this possible. People were thinking in a new way—a way that was colder, and more mathy—and that bound life and death up with money.

Insurance and annuities were a way of recapturing some (but not all) of the reciprocity that was present in small, pre-money societies. Because lots of ministers paid life insurance premiums and lived long lives, there was money to support the wives and children of the ministers who died young. Today, almost every rich society on Earth has some kind of social insurance—like, say, Social Security in the United States. Because millions of workers put a little money into the pot from every paycheck, millions of people who are too old to work get to take a little money out.

Probabilistic thinking has become so ubiquitous we've almost stopped noticing it. Insurance, of course, is still built on probability. But so are finance and business and sports and politics and medicine. We've come to take as given the revolutionary idea that we can predict the future.

CHAPTER 5

Finance as Time Travel: Inventing the Stock Market

It's a stretch to say that modern capitalism was invented in Amsterdam in the space of a few years in the early 1600s. But only a little bit of a stretch.

At the time, Europeans were really into sailing around the world and getting rich trading and stealing stuff from faraway lands. The Dutch were sending ships south around Africa and over to modern-day Indonesia and bringing back spices like nutmeg and mace. (Nutmeg and mace were huge in 1600; rich people paid absurd amounts to stock their spice drawers.)

But as Dutch merchants tried to send ships out for dangerous, multi-year voyages, they came up against a classic problem. They had a plan to make tons of money, but they had to spend a ton to put the plan in action. They had to build or buy ships, recruit a captain and a crew, and then send the ships and the captain and the crew around the world and back. There are infinite versions of this need-money-to-make-money problem: I want to buy a car, so I can drive to my new job, so I can make more money. But I need the money that I'm going to make at my new job now, so I can pay for the car, so I can drive to work, so I can make the money.

Fortunately, there are other people who have more money than they need right now. And they are willing to give up spending that money now so that they can have the chance of getting even more money later. This is how I can get a car loan, and how the Dutch got money to send ships to Asia, and it is one of the fundamentally useful things finance does: matches people who are willing to give up money now for the possibility of more money later with people who need money now and are willing to pay back more money later. Finance moves money around in time. "The essence of finance is time travel," the banker-turned-writer Matt Levine wrote. "Saving is about moving resources from the present into the future; financing is about moving resources from the future back into the present."

Those early voyages to the Spice Islands were usually financed as one-off deals. A bunch of rich people would pool their money to pay for a ship. If the ship made it all the way to Indonesia and back with a fortune in spices (no sure thing), then the investors would get their money back, with a profit on top. If the ship didn't make it back, thanks for playing—and oh, by the way, can we interest you in our next opportunity?

The Spanish, the Portuguese, and the British were all fighting for a piece of the Spice Islands action. It was a mix of business and imperialism and war, and the scattered Dutch ships financed by merchants were starting to look outmatched. So in 1602, the Dutch government created this new thing countries were trying: a trading company. Its formal name was the Vereenigde Oostindische Compagnie (United East India Company), or the VOC for short.

The government granted the VOC a monopoly on all Dutch

trade in Asia. The English had done something similar two years before, creating their own East India Company. But the Dutch East India Company would evolve in a way that would make it the first modern multinational corporation—the predecessor of Coca-Cola and Google and ExxonMobil.

People didn't have to be rich or well connected to invest in the VOC. "All the residents of these lands may buy shares in this Company," the charter said. This was in keeping with the spirit of the times. The Dutch had broken free from the King of Spain just a few decades earlier and formed a republic. It wasn't anything like a democracy in the modern sense, but power was much more widely distributed in the Netherlands than in monarchies of the time. A huge range of people invested in the VOC—over 1,000 people in Amsterdam alone, including the maid of one of the directors of the company, who put in ten months' salary.

At the time, companies everywhere could only be created by the explicit consent of the government, and they were always created to end after a fixed amount of time. The government gave the VOC a charter to operate for twenty-one years. Investors had the option of cashing out after ten years, but even that was a long time to wait. So in Amsterdam the directors of the VOC added a single line to the first page of the company register, the book where they recorded everyone's investments: "conveyance or transfer may be done through the bookkeeper of this chamber." In other words, if you want your money back before ten years have passed, you can sell your investment, your share of the company, to anyone who wants to buy it. This one line had a huge impact—not just on the VOC, but on the whole history of money.

People started selling their shares even before the first ship sailed. It wasn't particularly convenient; to execute a sale, the buyer and the seller both had to go to the company office, where a book-keeper had to record the deal in the register. But there were share-holders who needed money urgently, and nonshareholders who were willing to give up money now for the possibility of more money later. People who wanted to find buyers or sellers went to a bridge that ship captains crossed to deliver the mail when they came back from overseas. That made it the perfect place to get market-moving news before anyone else in town. Within a few years, there were so many traders on the bridge that they were blocking traffic. So the city commissioned a new building, just for trading—a courtyard 200 feet long by 115 feet wide, and surrounded by a covered gallery tiled in blue stone. It was the world's first stock exchange.

Five days before the exchange opened, the city passed a new ordinance, which said the exchange would only be allowed to be open a few hours a day—from 11 a.m. to noon, and again in the evening for an hour before dusk (thirty minutes in the winter). The limited hours sound like a pain, but there was a good reason for making this rule. If the market had been open all day, buyers and sellers would have trickled in and out. The spread between the price buyers were offering and the price sellers were asking would have been wide. People would have had to either make deals they didn't want to make or go without trading at all. This is what economists call a "thin market." The limited hours forced all potential buyers and sellers to show up at the same time—they turned the exchange into a "thick market," where hundreds or even thousands of peo-ple would show up to trade at the same time. This made it easier for buyers and sellers to find each other and agree on a price both thought was fair. It made the market work better.

As the VOC's charter was renewed, and renewed again, the stock exchange became an institution. A local merchant-poet named

Joseph de la Vega wrote a book about Amsterdam's stock market. It was the first book ever written about a stock market, and it had the perfect name for a book about the market: *Confusion of Confusions*.

The book is full of weird digressions into classical mythology and biblical analogies. But the descriptions of the stock exchange are shockingly familiar:

> *A member of the Exchange opens his hand and another takes it, and thus sells a number of shares at a fixed price, which is confirmed by a second handshake.... The handshakes are followed by shouting, the shouting by insults, the insults by impudence and more insults, shouting, pushes, and handshakes until the business is finished...*

Almost as soon as people started trading stocks, they also started coming up with complex variations that allowed for new kinds of bets. One kind of bet in particular emerged almost immediately: a short, which allows an investor to profit when the price of the stock goes down. People in Amsterdam hated shorts, as people around the world have continued to hate them ever since.

Short Story

The story of the first stock short in the history of the world explains the hate—but also why shorting is socially useful and wildly underrated.

Isaac Le Maire was a Dutch merchant, a founder of the VOC, and the single biggest shareholder in Amsterdam. A few years into the life of the company, Le Maire got into a fight with the other directors. The details are obscure, but it seems that he had financed part of an expedition, and the company didn't pay him back what he said he was owed. Le Maire may have inflated his expenses to defraud the company. There was a lawsuit; the directors froze Le Maire's shares. Le Maire left Amsterdam, holed up in the countryside, and plotted his revenge.

To get back at the VOC, Le Maire used a technique that local grain dealers had been using for a long time. Two people would agree to a sale at a certain price at a set date in the future. So, for example, one merchant might promise to buy a bushel of wheat for 100 guilders a year from today. This is called a futures contract, and today people make trillions of dollars in deals in contracts like these.

Working secretly through a team of confederates, Le Maire started entering into futures contracts for VOC stock. In October 1608 a trader working with Le Maire made a deal with an Amsterdam diamond merchant. Le Maire's trader agreed to sell the diamond merchant a share of VOC stock for 145 guilders in one year's time. This meant that if the stock was trading below 145 when the contract came due, Le Maire could buy a share on the open market, turn around and immediately sell it to the diamond merchant at a profit. And the lower the price of the stock, the bigger Le Maire's profit. Le Maire made lots of deals like these, eventually entering into contracts for more shares than he actually owned. If the price of the stock went down a lot, he'd get rich. If it went up a lot, he'd be wiped out.

So Le Maire started trying to drive the price of the stock down. His confederates in Amsterdam spread rumors about problems with the VOC. The company was spending too much money. Ships were sinking and getting captured by the enemy. Profits weren't as high as everybody thought they'd be. Sure enough, the price of VOC shares started falling.

The directors of the company didn't know that Le Maire was involved, but they knew someone was betting on the price of shares falling, and heard the rumors about the company, and they knew that the price was falling. The VOC was a source of both national pride and international power for the Dutch. For the sake of the nation (and for the sake of the large personal fortunes the directors had invested in VOC shares), they decided to stop this attack on the company.

The directors appealed to lawmakers. They said there was a "dirty scheme" to bring down the price of shares and suggested foreign spies might be behind the whole thing. "The general enemy has its accomplices among the important sellers," they wrote. In case a dirty scheme perpetrated by the general enemy wasn't enough to get lawmakers' attention, the directors added that the victims included "the many widows and orphans" who owned VOC shares.

In the case of enemy spies (the people betting against the VOC) versus widows and orphans (the shareholders), the Dutch legislature did what every legislature in the history of the world would have done. It did something, anything, to make it look like it was on the side of widows and orphans. In February 1610, the lawmakers banned investors from promising to sell in the future any shares they did not possess in the present. Put another way, they made Le Maire's scheme illegal.

The price of VOC stock started rising almost immediately. Several of Le Maire's partners went bankrupt. Le Maire lost tons of money. His scheme failed. The directors got their happy ending.

But! What if Team Le Maire was telling the truth about the VOC? What if there was a good reason for the share price to fall?

When the government was trying to decide what to do about the people betting against the VOC, a group of share dealers (which may have included Le Maire's partners) argued that the share price was falling because the business wasn't being run very well. It "is widely known and clear to everyone that many more ships are being sent than is necessary," they wrote. Le Maire wrote a letter to a senior government official, adding up the cost of all the VOC ships that had run aground and disappeared. And those ships that did make it back were bringing too much of a spice called mace, and not enough other stuff. All that mace was sitting unsold in warehouses, deteriorating in quality. The people betting against the stock, according to Le Maire, were just investors "who engage in some buying and selling of shares…on the basis of the news and information that they receive on a daily basis." The directors, Le Maire said, had bought "large portions of shares at a very high price." They weren't trying to ban shorts to protect widows and orphans. They were doing it to enrich themselves.

Today, if the price of a stock suddenly starts falling, it's routine for the CEO of the company to go on TV and say the people betting against the stock are spreading rumors. People's retirements are invested in our company! Think of the widows and orphans! Everybody wants the market to go up; people betting stocks will fall seem like the bad guys.

But the point of the stock market is not to go up. The point of the stock market is to find the right price for stocks—the price that best reflects all available information about the performance of the company and the state of the world. Obviously, stock markets sometimes fail miserably at this task. But the more investors who are in the market—and, crucially, the more information they bring to the market—the better the market will be at finding the right price. Allowing people to profit when the price of a stock falls creates an incentive for investors to root out fraud and spread bad news that might otherwise remain unnoticed. This is a good thing.

Isaac Le Maire kept arguing with the authorities over money he claimed he was owed. They never gave it to him. He died in a small town by the sea and was buried under a tombstone with this epitaph:

> Here lies Isaac Le Maire, merchant, who, during his activities over all the parts of the world, by the grace of God, knew so much abundance that in thirty years he lost (save his honour) more than 150,000 florins.

This may be the only tombstone on Earth that brags about how much money the deceased lost. Also, it seems to be a typo. In a letter written before he died, Le Maire mentioned losing 1,600,000 florins. His epitaph is missing a zero.

CHAPTER 6

John Law Gets to Print Money

Even booming Amsterdam had its own version of the money problem. In this case, the problem was not a shortage of coins, like in Britain. It was too many different kinds of coins.

Traders and merchants from all over Europe were doing business in Amsterdam. They often used written promises to pay, which were sort of like postdated checks, and were known as bills of exchange. But when it came time to settle a bill—to make payment in real silver and gold—things got messy. All these foreign traders had coins from different countries and kingdoms and city-states, so Amsterdam's city government assigned official values to almost 1,000 different coins. There were counterfeits, and some coins had been shaved and didn't weigh as much as they were supposed to. Sometimes traders literally had to haggle over every coin. This was a boon for money changers, and for hustlers, but it was a drag on honest merchants who just wanted to do business without worrying about every coin.

So in 1609, just a few years after the VOC was created, the city of Amsterdam chartered a public bank—a bank owned not by money changers or investors, but by the city itself. The purpose of the bank was not to make a profit, but to solve Amsterdam's money problem. Along with the bank came a new law that said if you had bills of exchange coming due in Amsterdam, you had to go to the bank to settle up.

Merchants opened accounts at the bank. When a bill came due, they could pay it (or get paid) simply by having the bank transfer money out of (or into) their account by changing the numbers in the bank's ledgers. They didn't have to worry about all those different coins anymore, or about counterfeits. The account at the bank—the number on the bank's ledger—was their money. And it worked better than coins.

As John Law gambled his way through Europe, he saw Amsterdam getting rich because it had a bank that created reliable money for everyone to use, and a stock market where anyone could invest, and colonies on the other side of the world (like a lot of his European contemporaries, Law was apparently not troubled by the atrocities committed by the colonialists). At some point, John Law had a vision. He would stop wandering around Europe. He would go back to Scotland—not as a gambler or a convicted murderer, but as a hero bringing economic revolution.

By the time Law went back to Scotland, he was in his early thirties and had been wandering around Europe for about a decade. He got home and started trying to convince his countrymen that they were screwing themselves with their rickety financial system where there was never enough money. In 1705, he published a 120-page pamphlet called "Money and Trade Considered, With a Proposal for Supplying the Nation With Money." (His aunt was the publisher.)

He pointed to the Dutch and said, there are all these reasons they should have a crappy country.

Their natural Disadvantages are, smalness of Territory, barrenness of Soil...want of Mines; long Winters; unwholsome Air;...a dangerous Coast;

difficult Entry to their Rivers; the Sea to defend against on one side, and power-
ful Neighbours on the other . . .

But despite all that, the Dutch prospered because they solved the money problem.

. . . they are become a rich and powerful People.

Scotland, Law continued, was in exactly the opposite situation.

Scotland has by Nature many Advantages for Trade; a large Territory; of easie defence; plenty of People; a wholsome Air; Mines . . .; a safe Coast; Rivers of easie Entry; the Seas and Rivers stockt with Fish. . . .

Scotland just had to solve its money problem.

Scotland needed to create more money. The creation of money would make it cheaper for people to borrow and invest, and it would create jobs for the unemployed. This is basic, uncontroversial monetary policy today; back then it was the moon. To create more money, he continued, Scotland needed to get over its outdated ideas and create a government-chartered bank, like the one in Amsterdam. But Scotland should go further. The new bank, Law argued, should print paper money that was backed not by silver or gold, but by land. That way, Scotland could have a lot more money, even without getting more gold or silver.

Scotland's parliament debated whether to take Law's advice. The head of one party called Law's ideas "a contrivance to enslave the nation." An earl from an opposing party defended the ideas. The party head challenged the earl to a duel (always with the duel). The men met on the edge of town; excuses ensued; pistols were fired into the air. The duel was over, and no one was hurt, but Law's chance of changing Scotland was dead. Not long after, it became clear that Scotland and England were about to unite into Great Britain, and John Law, still wanted for murder in England, had to go back on the lam.

Again he wandered through Europe. But this time, instead of

just gambling, he was dreaming of solving the money problems of an entire nation—any nation would do. He pitched his ideas to the Austrian emperor, who didn't bite (though Law apparently did well at the gambling tables of Vienna). He tried and failed to sell the Duke of Savoy on a Bank of Turin. In 1714, Law moved to Paris, where he struck local officials as sketchy. The chief of police warned the foreign minister:

> A Scot named Law, gambler by profession and suspected of evil intentions towards the King, appears at Paris in high style and has even bought an impressive home...although no one knows of any resource except fortune in gambling, which is his whole profession.

But in Paris Law finally caught a break. In the margin of the letter, the foreign minister wrote of Law: "He is not suspect. He may be left in peace."

By this time, Law had a common-law wife (who had never formally divorced her first husband, nor married Law, but whatever, it's France) and two kids. He was super rich (he kept a lot of his money in the Bank of Amsterdam) and bought a mansion on a fashionable square in Paris where the Ritz Hotel stands today. He had a collection of paintings by Italian masters and what the suspicious police chief described as a "sizeable retinue of servants."

Maybe most important, Law had become good friends with the Duke of Orléans, a debauched French nobleman who was about to become very important. The Duke's hobbies included working in his home chemistry lab, composing operas, and staying up all night with nobles and opera singers and actresses who got drunk, slept with each other, and "said vile things at the tops of their voices." The Duke's big moment came in September 1715, when King Louis the XIV died.

The heir, Louis XV, was five years old. Orléans was appointed Regent, which meant he got to rule France until the boy king came of age.

He took over a bankrupt country. The previous king—which is to say the French government—had borrowed everywhere he could, mostly to fund a never-ending series of wars. He'd forced people to turn in their silver coins to be re-minted for a fee. People responded by hoarding their coins or by smuggling them out of the country to somewhere safer, like Amsterdam. At one point the king got so desperate he melted down his own silver furniture to turn it into coins. Then he borrowed some more, promising his lenders that they could keep all of the country's tax revenues for years to come.

Everyone in France with money to loan had loaned to the government. When the government didn't pay them back, they couldn't pay their own debts. By the end of Louis XIV's reign, the economy had collapsed entirely. "The shortage of credit was universal, trade was destroyed, consumption was cut by half, the cultivation of lands neglected, the people unhappy," a minister wrote.

Law was forty-four years old. He'd been pitching his ideas about money for a decade. Finally, with his buddy as the Regent, he was about to get his big chance.

It's Money If Everyone Believes It's Money

During the twenty years John Law had been on the lam, England, the former financial backwater, had leapt ahead of every other country in Europe by solving the problem the king of France and, really, every king and every government has always faced: how to raise money.

Governments did then what governments do now—they taxed

people, and they borrowed. But Europe's monarchies tended to tax and borrow in a sort of random, ad hoc way. One year, the king would have a big, one-off lottery. (Like a tax, but more fun!) The next, maybe sell a few annuities and borrow from the rich. Maybe he'd pay them back, maybe he wouldn't.

In 1694, the English tried to solve the government money problem in a new way. They had just gone through a revolution in which Parliament demanded limits on the power of the monarch. Now Parliament and the newly installed king and queen took all of these new money technologies that were starting to take off—banks and stocks and paper money—and created a new kind of bank. They called it the Bank of England.

The first thing the bank did was sell shares to raise £1.2 million from investors. These people weren't depositing money in the bank. They were buying shares as an investment, the same way you can buy stock in Bank of America or Wells Fargo on the New York Stock Exchange today.

As with the Dutch East India Company (the VOC), which was now nearly one hundred years old, anybody who wanted to could invest. And everybody wanted to invest. Merchants and farmers and sailors and vicars all got in on it. The king and queen kicked in £10,000, which was the maximum allowed. Eleven days after the bank started accepting investments, it had raised the £1.2 million. The last investor was one Judith Shirley, of Sussex, who put in £75.

The bank, in turn, loaned that £1.2 million to the king, who promised to pay 8 percent a year interest. And that wasn't just the king saying he was good for it. The same act of Parliament that created the bank also created a special, new tax on shipping that the government was legally required to use to pay the interest on the loan.

The bank's loan to the king was not in the form of gold and

silver coins. The bank gave the king paper notes redeemable for gold and silver at the bank. The king used the money to fund a war.

The Bank of England was a huge success. It created a new, safe way for ordinary people to trade some money now for the possibility of more money later. They could lend, through the bank, to the government, in a regular, predictable way, and the law promised they'd be paid back. And because the bank was lending out more money than it had in the vaults, it created more money for England as a whole, in a way that was much more stable and reliable than a few random goldsmiths giving people claim checks.

By 1715, John Law had cooked up a plan to take what the Bank of England had done and push it much, much further.

When Law closed his eyes, he could see a whole financial system that linked together all of the hot new things—a bank, a stock market, a trading company, a new way for the government to get money. In a letter to the Duke of Orléans, who now ruled France as Regent, Law described the system with characteristic modesty:

> But the bank is not the only nor the greatest of my ideas. I will produce a work that will surprise Europe by the changes it will bring in France's favor, greater changes than those brought by the discovery of the Indies or by the introduction of credit. By this work Your Royal Highness will be in a position to relieve the kingdom of the sad condition into which it has fallen, and to make it more powerful than it has ever been...

Law persuaded the Regent to let him start the first full-fledged bank in France. It had a big name—the Banque Générale—but it was so small that it was based in Law's house. Like the Bank of England, Law's bank raised money by selling stock to investors. Unlike the Bank of England, almost nobody wanted in. The French establishment made fun of Law's little bank. One writer called it "a vision…one can only laugh at it, no one believes it will last." Both John Law and the institution of banking seemed weird and foreign and generally untrustworthy.

But Law believed. He believed so hard he bought a quarter of the shares in the bank. Perhaps more important, Law's old drinking buddy Orléans, who happened to be running France, also believed. And in the summer of 1716, Orléans sent chests full of gold from the Royal Mint to the Banque Générale—and made sure everybody knew about it. A Paris magazine described "an order the other day from the mint to send a million to M. Law's bank, that the Regent supports and is really his bank under the name of this Englishman. Everyone believes that it will hold up because royal funds are going in to it."

Remember the first seven words of that last sentence: "Everyone believes that it will hold up." They are the essence of banking (and, for that matter, of money). If everyone believes a bank will hold up, it will almost certainly hold up. If, on the other hand, people think a bank is going to fail, it will fail—even if its finances are in great shape.

The Duke's big deposit ensured Law's bank's survival. The bank's big break came the next year, in 1717, when the Regent made a new rule that forced everyone in Paris and the surrounding areas to use paper notes issued by the bank to pay their taxes.

A pretty good working definition of money is: it's the thing you pay taxes with. In a world where different things are competing to be money—bills of exchange, silver and gold coins, notes from private banks—the thing the government accepts for taxes is going to win. It's going to become money. That's what happened in Paris in 1717. When the Regent forced people to use paper to pay their taxes, John Law's paper became money. Now that Law's paper was money, he was ready to go big.

CHAPTER 7

The Invention of Millionaires

By the early eighteenth century, the Netherlands and England and Spain and Portugal had been sailing around the world for hundreds of years, looting and pillaging and harvesting cinnamon and getting rich. Starting in the sixteenth century, the French launched a series of expeditions to North America and managed to claim a good-sized chunk of present-day Canada and roughly half of the continental United States in a territory centered on the Mississippi River. (The French, of course, didn't ask permission from the Native Americans who had lived there for thousands of years.)

Right around the time the Regent made everybody in Paris start using Law's banknotes to pay their taxes, he also agreed to charter a second endeavor of Law's. It was officially called the Company of the West, but everybody called it the Mississippi Company. The French government granted the company a monopoly on all of France's trade along the Mississippi River. It was going to be like the Dutch East India Company (the VOC), only better.

Law promised that the Mississippi Company was going to help the Regent deal with all that debt the previous king had run up.

The debt was in the form of bonds: rich French people had loaned the king money, and in exchange they had received the king's promise that he would repay them the loan, plus 4 percent interest a year. But those interest payments had become a burden. So Law would allow French investors to trade in their bonds for shares in the Mississippi Company. Then the company would collect the debt from the king, but at a lower rate of interest over a longer period of time. This would reduce the interest payments for the government but still provide a stream of income for Law's company.

Law made his pitch to the wealthy bondholders. What would you rather have, he asked them, unreliable payments of 4 percent interest from a dodgy boy-king or all the riches in the New World?

The French chose 4 percent interest. As with Law's bank, almost nobody wanted in on his trading company. So, once again, Law and the Duke of Orléans poured in their own money.

Slowly, though, things started happening. In the spring of 1718, a colonist working for the company founded a new capital, near the mouth of the Mississippi River. He wanted to flatter the Regent, so he named the capital after him: New Orleans.

Back in France, Law's persistence was finally beginning to pay off. People found that they liked using Law's paper money—it was, in fact, easier to use than gold or silver. Within a few years, the bank had several branches around the country, which allowed people to move money from town to town simply by going to their local bank branch and requesting a transfer. And by making loans and creating money, Law's bank did seem to be giving the French economy a useful boost. The basic business of growing food and making stuff started working again in France.

"The Talk Was All of Millions"

In December 1718, Law's bank became the Banque Royale—the Royal Bank. It was now controlled entirely by the king (which is to say, by Law's pal Orléans). The new charter said the bank could print as much paper money as the king allowed. It also formally linked the ownership of the bank and the Mississippi Company. More paper money would lead to more trade, which would make everybody better off. The bank and the company would support each other, and all of France (and of course John Law) would be richer for it.

Things started happening fast. In the next few months, Law merged the Mississippi Company with other French companies that were supposed to be trading with Asia and Africa but hadn't really been doing much. Law also acquired the right to trade tobacco in France. ("They call it the magic plant, because those who begin to use it can no longer give it up," the Regent's mother, Princess Palatine, said.)

To pay for these acquisitions, Law planned to sell new shares in the Mississippi Company. People saw that the company was growing, and they had money in their pockets—money that Law's bank was printing. Everybody wanted to buy shares. Here Law made a genius move. He said: you can't buy the new shares unless you already own the old shares. So everybody rushed to buy the old shares, and the price started shooting up.

A few weeks later, the Company bought the rights to all the profits from the Royal Mint for the next nine years. Law financed that with another generation of shares—and to buy shares this time, you had to own both of the previous generations of shares. The share price went up some more.

By August 1719, shares were trading for more than 3,000 livres each, up from around 500 a few months earlier. Around this time, Law made his biggest move yet. He offered to lend the king enough money to pay off the entire national debt of France. He was basically offering to consolidate the king's loans: take all of these different loans, bundle them all together, and lower the interest rate the king had to pay. The king—in the person of the Regent—accepted Law's offer. To raise the money, Law sold more stock.

People knew the price was only going to go up after the stock hit the open market, so they went straight to Law to try to get stock directly from him. "Law was continually besieged by suppliants and flatterers; his door was forced, people entered by the windows from his garden, and fell down the chimney into his study," a nobleman wrote at the time. "The talk was all of millions." The word *millionaire* was invented to describe the people who were getting rich off their Mississippi Company stock.

Law kept swallowing up more and more of the business of the French state. Eventually, inevitably, the Regent granted Law the right to collect taxes on behalf of the king. The French had special taxes on every little thing people bought. Law replaced those with a single income tax, which was more efficient and less of a burden for the poor. "The people went dancing and jumping about the street, as if they were distracted for joy," Daniel Defoe wrote from Paris that fall. "They now pay not one farthing tax for wood, coal, hay, oats, oil, wine, beer, bread, cards, soap, cattle, fish, or, in a word, for anything...."

France boomed. Money was everywhere. In the countryside, farmers started growing food on land that had lain fallow. In Paris, artisans sold more lace, and plates, and clothes than ever. The government hired workers to build roads and bridges. French soldiers were off fighting Spain—they were always off fighting somebody—but this time, the government could pay them without melting down the king's silverware.

John Law was, increasingly, the French economy. He collected taxes for the government and received the government's payment on the national debt. He had a monopoly on all of France's trade outside Europe. And he could literally print money.

The Mississippi Company stock kept rising. Hundreds of thousands of people from all over Europe came to Paris to get in on the action. They crowded around the company's office to get the latest news, and to buy and sell shares. Carriages couldn't get through, so city officials closed the street to traffic and put iron gates on either end. Every day at 7 a.m. they rang a bell and banged a drum and opened the gates, and everyone rushed in to buy and sell stock. A clerk at the British embassy wrote that the street "is crowded from early in the morning to late at night with princes and princesses, dukes and peers and duchesses etc. in a word all that is great in France. They sell estates and pawn jewels to purchase Mississippi." Law's footman (the guy who rides on the back of the carriage) got so rich on Company stock that he quit his job and hired two footmen—one for himself and one for Law. In early December, shares hit 10,000.

The shares of the Company Law bought when no one wanted them now made him, a man on the run from a murder charge in England, the wealthiest non-royal in Europe. He bought a dozen country estates, several mansions in Paris, a bunch of diamonds, and 45,000 books.

In January 1720, Law was appointed Controller-General of Finances for all of France—the second most powerful job in the country after the Regent. The job gave John Law very high status, which paired nicely with all that wealth. The government thanked him for "the important services that you have rendered to our State as much for the establishment of our Royal Bank, whose utility we appreciate, as for the different arrangements that have been made for the payment of our public debts, for the increase in our state revenues and the relief of our people."

The Real Economy Versus the Mississippi Bubble

A share in the Mississippi Company, just like a share of Apple, or GM, or any other corporation today, entitled its owner to a share of all the company's future profits, forever. The run-up in the Mississippi Company's share price between 1719 and 1720 was based on the promise of vast future profits. This seemed plausible enough. The Spanish had discovered a mountain full of silver in South America, and the Dutch grew rich controlling remote islands full of cinnamon and cloves. There were stories in France of the great riches of the Mississippi territory: an emerald mountain, vast silver deposits, hundreds of prosperous houses springing up in New Orleans.

In fact, there were no emeralds or silver. By 1719, French settlers had built a total of four houses in New Orleans. But Law seems to have really believed there was potential for something great. The company bought dozens of ships, and Law invested his own money to send settlers to an area west of the Mississippi, in what is now Arkansas, to grow tobacco and look for silver. Most of them died of disease and starvation, which was what usually happened when Europeans went there. People from around Europe flocked to Paris to get rich trading Mississippi Company stock; they did not flock to Mississippi. So Law pushed through new laws for transporting army deserters, prostitutes, and criminals to America, and in 1719 ships of unwilling settlers started sailing across the Atlantic. It was a desperation move; things weren't going well.

In March 1720, John Law made a shocking announcement—one that would ultimately doom his whole project. He said the Mississippi Company would buy or sell unlimited quantities of company stock at the fixed price of 9,000 livres, just below where the stock was trading on the open market. It seems like he wanted to stop the run-up in prices and stabilize the market. What ended up happening was lots of people sold their stock back to the company. And the bank (now owned by the company) printed more paper money to buy all the stock.

Economists have this odd phrase: "the real economy." It means, roughly, all economic activity that happens outside of finance. The carpenter who builds your house works in the real economy. The banker who lends you money to buy the house does not. When an economy is working well, the real economy and finance support each other. The banker gives you a loan so you can buy the house the carpenter built. Everyone (theoretically) wins.

But there are times when the real economy and finance become disconnected. Sometimes, finance lags behind the real economy. There's not enough money, or loans, to go around, and nobody wants to invest in anything. That was France before John Law got there. (The Great Depression is the classic example from the modern era.)

At other times, finance races out ahead of the real economy. There's too much money floating around, it's too easy to get a loan, and everybody wants to invest. People start buying not because they want a future stream of income from their investments, but because they speculate they can turn around and sell for more in a day or a month. That was France in 1720—and it was turning into a problem for the real economy. All that new money floating around was driving up the price of basic staples like wheat, candles, and milk. From the fall of 1719 to the fall of 1720, prices nearly doubled.

Law knew he needed to take money out of circulation to bring the financial economy back in line with the real economy. He believed in paper money—he'd been preaching that gospel for fifteen years. And he thought if he could get people to stop using gold and silver as money, he could both stabilize the economy and, finally, break the link between precious metal and money.

In the first months of 1720 he made it illegal to possess large amounts of gold or silver coins. Suddenly everybody had lots of new gold and silver jewelry. So Law made it illegal to produce any gold object bigger than one ounce, except for crosses and ceremonial chalices. This prompted an immediate outbreak of piety in Paris; big gold crosses were the new new thing. Law banned big gold crosses.

As the jewelers were getting rich, Law was starting to lose his grip. He pushed through a series of measures that required people to use paper money for all large purchases. Then he said that, by the end of the year, people would no longer be able to exchange their banknotes for gold and silver. Paper money would just be paper.

In May 1720, Law went further. He declared the value of paper money would be gradually cut in half. At this point, France flipped out. People rioted for three days. The bank closed. People threw rocks through the windows.

A week later, the Regent overruled Law and revoked the order. But it didn't matter anymore. The system was in freefall. People crowded the streets of Paris, not to trade Mississippi stock but to exchange their paper money for silver. The bank, of course, didn't have enough silver. Farmers stopped accepting paper money.

Law was fired, then rehired, then fired again. In an echo of what happened hundreds of years earlier in China, the Regent gave up on paper money, and on banks entirely. The government went back to gold and silver coins and took on new debts to compensate people who had lost money on Mississippi stock and paper notes. It was as if Law had never existed.

Law was placed under house arrest. Mobs attacked his house and his coach. His only choice was to flee France, as he had fled England twenty-five years earlier. In December he took a borrowed coach to Brussels, where he stayed under an assumed name, which didn't matter, because everybody knew who he was anyway, so he went to the theater and, weirdly, got a standing ovation. He went to England, where he kneeled before a panel of judges and was pardoned for killing Beau Wilson in that duel decades earlier.

He kept writing to Orléans, asking to be allowed back. He still believed in his system; he said he could fix everything. Orléans might have eventually agreed, but he died of a heart attack in 1723 at age forty-nine. He was with his mistress at the time.

Eventually, Law settled in Venice with his son. His common-law wife and his daughter were still in France; he would never see them again. Most of Law's money was stuck in France, so he lived once again by gambling. He won enough to survive, but he didn't get rich; creditors were after him until he died in March 1729, just before his fifty-eighth birthday.

✳ ✳ ✳

In late 1720, just as the wheels were coming off the French economy, a Dutch artist published a series of cartoons about what was happening in France. My favorite shows three men pouring gold coins down Law's throat in a street crowded with people. Law is squatting, and his butt is bare, and a piece of paper is coming out of it. A man in the crowd is grabbing the paper.

Credit: The Granger Collection

This, more or less, has become the standard view of what the French call John Law's System and the English call the Mississippi Bubble. Law took all the money and gave France crap in return. He was running a long con, and in the end he was found out.

I don't buy this view. In 1716, when John Law was first pitching his bank, Orléans went to one of his closest advisors, the Duke of Saint-Simon, to ask him what he thought. Saint-Simon told him that Law's ideas made sense. Paper money could be good for France's economy. But, Saint-Simon said, there was a problem. Unlike the Netherlands, which was a republic, or Great Britain, which had a powerful Parliament, France was an absolute monarchy. The king could do whatever he wanted. And inevitably, the king or the people working for him would get carried away by the power of the bank, and they'd print too much money, and the system would break.

For modern money to work—to have banks, and a stock market, and a central bank—there needs to be tension. Investors and bankers and activists and government officials all need to be arguing over who gets to do what, and when. Often today, the people making those arguments suggest the system is broken: The government is interfering too much or the bankers are getting away with murder. But those arguments themselves are, if not sufficient to make the system work, at least necessary. The push and pull among people with different interests—lenders and borrowers, investors and workers—is what keeps money stable. Economic historians have argued that the Bank of England and paper money took off in England when they did in large part because Parliament had just gained power relative to the king. People were more likely to lend money to the government because they thought Parliament would keep the king in line.

John Law's System wasn't inherently flawed; John Law was inherently flawed. He failed because he wanted too much power—and when he got it, the power structure in France meant there was no one to push back, no way to create that necessary balance.

"The founding of a national bank would be fatal in an absolute monarchy," Saint-Simon said just before Law founded his bank, "whereas in a free country it might be a wise and profitable undertaking."

III

MORE MONEY

Money feels finite. It feels like there's only so much to go around; if some-one is getting more, someone else must be getting less. In most places at most times, this was mostly true. But then, in the decades after John Law's death, something changed—apparently forever, or at least so far.

Now, everyone can have more money. Chapter 8 is, in an oblique way, the story of this transformation. Chapter 9 is about the more intuitive but less rosy corollary: just because everybody can have more money, it doesn't mean everybody will have more money.

CHAPTER 8

Everybody Can Have More Money

For most of human history, the world was a dark place. The cost of lighting was so profoundly high that when the sun went down people often just huddled in their shack or hut and waited for dawn.

The story of how we got from huddling in the dark to having as much light as we want at the flick of a switch explains a ridiculous amount about the world. It explains why most people on Earth no longer have to worry constantly about starving to death. It explains why most people aren't subsistence farmers—why we can have a world of people who make their living as personal trainers and HR professionals and plumbers. It explains climate change. It also explains why the amount of money in the world is not fixed, why one person's gain is not another's loss, why everybody can have more money.

Toward the end of the twentieth century, Bill Nordhaus, an economist at Yale, became obsessed with the history of light. He knew that light is a thing society has needed forever. And he realized that if he really understood the economics of artificial light, he would understand how to measure the history of material progress.

The puzzle Nordhaus set out to solve was this: How has the price of artificial light changed over the past, oh, say, 4,000 years? Price, for economists, is basically the center of the world. It is where the abstraction that is money meets reality.

Nordhaus decided to start his research in ancient Babylon (a city in Mesopotamia, the same region where accountants invented writing). To figure out what Babylonians paid for light, Nordhaus bought an ancient-style oil lamp. The Babylonians, conveniently enough, used sesame oil to fuel their lamps. So Nordhaus bought some sesame oil at the grocery store. He borrowed a light meter from a guy in the facilities department at Yale. Then he put the lamp on his dining room table, lit it, and measured how much light the lamp put out, and how long it took to burn through a quarter cup of sesame oil.

From another scholar, Nordhaus got figures for how much workers earned in ancient Babylon, and how much sesame oil cost. Then he did some math that allowed him to make the price of artificial light comparable across all of human history. Eventually, he could answer this question: If you were a typical worker in ancient Babylon and you spent a whole day's earnings on light, how long could you illuminate a small room with as much light as you get today from a 60-watt incandescent lightbulb?

Ten minutes! A day of work only got you ten minutes of light!

In ancient Babylon, it took a lot of hours of human labor to grow sesame seeds. It took a lot of hours to press those seeds into oil. As a result, sesame oil—and, more to the point, the light you got by burning sesame oil—was really expensive.

Over time, around the world, people made light any way they could. In the Caribbean and in parts of Asia, people made lanterns

5 hours of light

4

3

2

1

10 minutes

Ancient Babylon

Source: Bill Nordhaus

Credit: Quoctrung Bui

out of fireflies. In parts of Great Britain, people took (dead) birds called storm petrels, stuck wicks down their throats, and turned them into candles.

But for the most part, for thousands of years, artificial light was expensive and the world stayed dark. This may sound sort of romantic—the moonlight, the stars!—but for a lot of people, a lot of the time, the dark was awful. The dark was not some beautiful thing you went out and explored. It was something dangerous. Something that trapped you. In Paris at one point, there was actually a law that said, every night, everybody had to give their keys to a magistrate, go home, and lock themselves in the house.

By the 1700s, a new fuel source for light was becoming widespread: whale oil. This was very, very bad for whales. But it did mean light got cheaper and better. When Nordhaus crunched the numbers for Europe in the 1700s, here's what he found.

Everybody Can Have More Money   79

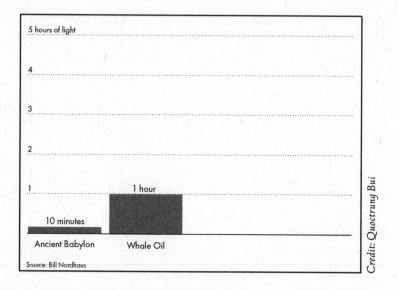

5 hours of light

4

3

2

1 hour

1

10 minutes

Ancient Babylon   Whale Oil

Source: Bill Nordhaus

Credit: Quoctrung Bui

Things definitely got better for people (and tragically worse for whales). Humanity had gone from a day's labor buying ten minutes of light to a day's labor buying an hour. But it took 4,000 years to make that gain!

In the 1700s, life everywhere on Earth still looked more like ancient Babylon than the modern world. People still traveled the same way—by foot, by horse, by sailing ship. Most people were still subsistence farmers, usually living in some kind of hut, trying to grow enough food to not starve to death.

Then, around 1800, everything changed. When you look at history, it's like there are two different economic universes: the universe before 1800 and what came after. This moment is the Industrial Revolution, which started with making steam power and cloth in Great Britain and spread to making everything everywhere. It's frankly not entirely clear why so much changed at this particular moment. But there are a couple things that are essential to the history of light.

One is, basically, practical applications of science. The important breakthrough wasn't that the Earth orbits the sun or how the force of gravity changes based on the distance between two objects; the breakthrough was discovering a system for making new discoveries, the scientific method. Not all of these discoveries had practical applications, but some did.

Around 1850, a scientist named Abraham Gesner (he was a physician who had also studied geology) discovered a new technique for turning pitch or oil into a fuel he called kerosene. It was an extraordinary breakthrough—it was just so much better than every light source that had come before. It was brighter, and cleaner, and much, much cheaper.

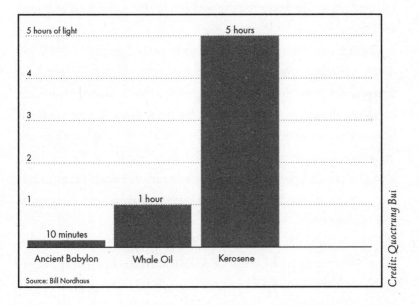

Credit: Quoctrung Bui

With kerosene, Nordhaus figured, a day's wages bought a European worker about five hours of light. In about fifty years, the amount of light a worker could buy rose fivefold—roughly the same amount it had risen in the four thousand years before that.

The Lightbulb Moment

Thomas Edison and the lightbulb—the big moment in the history of light—is, of course, partly a story about science and technology. But it's not only that. It's also a story about money.

In the 1870s, lots of people were trying to use electricity to make light. Inventors in the United States and France were working on a technology called arc lights—these big, superbright lights that hung from high poles. They worked as street lamps and lights in factories. But they were too big and too bright to be used in homes or offices.

Edison first went to see arc lights in early September 1878 and decided immediately that he could do better. But doing better—figuring out how to invent the lightbulb as we know it—would be expensive. Those stories of Edison spending years doing thousands of experiments to get the bulb right aren't entirely accurate in one important way—it wasn't just Edison alone in a room. By this time, he had a whole invention factory next to his house in Menlo Park, New Jersey, where he paid scribes and mechanics and machinists and blacksmiths to help him invent stuff.

Edison was rich and famous—he'd already invented the record player!—but even so, he knew he couldn't afford to invent the lightbulb on his own. He wrote to his lawyer, "All I want at present is to be provided with funds to push the light rapidly."

Fortunately for Edison, there was now a way for a promising inventor to quickly raise lots of money from lots of people: he could create a company. Companies were no longer just these things governments created to go do imperialism. Now they were for everybody.

On October 16, just a month and a half after Edison had seen the arc lights, the Edison Electric Light Company was created. It would eventually morph into General Electric—GE. Like many companies created then (and now), it was a limited liability corporation (an LLC). This meant investors could put money into the company and be guaranteed that, if it went bust, they would lose only the money they'd put in, not any of their personal wealth. This seems so obvious today that to even mention it is sort of confusing; of course you can't lose more than your investment. But for a long time, if you invested in a business, and that business owed people money, you were on the hook. The people the business owed money to could, say, seize your house to make good on the debts of the business you invested in. The corporation and the limited liability that went with it made it much easier for people like Edison to find willing investors.

In the weeks after the Edison Electric Light Company was created, investors rushed to put up $50,000 (about $1 million in today's money), giving Edison the money he needed to pay his team. Those investors hoped to become rich from another financial innovation that was essential to the explosion of invention around this time: patents. The point of patents—which the founders of America thought was so important they put it in the Constitution— is to give people a financial incentive to come up with new ideas, and to share those ideas with the world. A patent is a temporary, government-granted monopoly on new ideas. So if you come up with a new idea that lots of people are willing to pay for, you can make a lot of money. The investors in the Edison Electric Light company were promised a share of the profits from whatever electricity or lightbulb-related patents Edison was awarded.

Just over a year after his company was formed, Edison was awarded US patent 223,898 for the electric lamp, aka the lightbulb. He wasn't the only inventor working on lightbulbs, and there are disputes remaining today over who invented what when. But Edison went on to receive dozens more patents for lightbulbs and for ways to build an electrical grid to power those bulbs.

A few years later, Edison started building the first power grid— not just his first, but the first in the history of the world—in New York City. For this he needed lots more money, and he founded a whole other company to raise it. In September 1882, just four years after Edison saw arc lights and knew he could do better, someone flipped the switch at a new power plant and suddenly lightbulbs in homes and offices scattered around lower Manhattan glowed. It was like magic. But Edison wasn't at the power plant to flip the switch. He was a few blocks away, literally on Wall Street, hanging out with J. P. Morgan and a bunch of other bankers to witness this momentous occasion. It was money, as much as anything, that made the lights go on.

It wasn't all magic. The first power plants burned dirty coal, polluting the city. A few decades later, Edison built a huge power plant on the east side of Manhattan. At some point the city health department started sending inspectors. "When it was found health department men were trying to photograph the smokestacks," the *New York Times* reported, "scouts were put on the company's roof who ordered the feeding of coal stopped whenever photographers appeared."

Over time, though, power—and, with it, light—kept getting cheaper (and cleaner). A day's wages bought more and more. This was true not only about light, but about almost everything. The internal combustion engine led to tractors, which made farmers wildly more productive. Suddenly, for the first time in human history, most people didn't have to spend their lives trying to grow (or kill or find) food. This went on decade after decade, all through the twentieth century. All kinds of things got much cheaper.

Bill Nordhaus, the Yale economist, did his light study at the end of the twentieth century. By that time, if a typical worker spent a day's wages on light, here's how long they could light up a room:

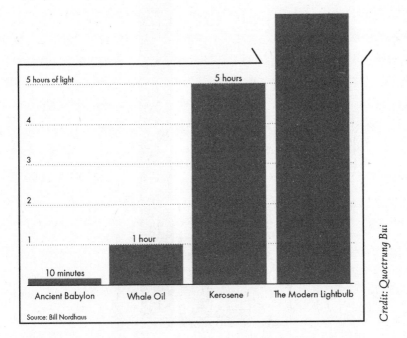

Credit: Quoctrung Bui

We need to zoom out a little here.

5 hours of light

4

3

2

1

10 minutes

Ancient Babylon

1 hour

Whale Oil

5 hours

Kerosene

The Modern Lightbulb

Source: Bill Nordhaus

Credit: Quoctrung Bui

Keep going. Zoom out a little more...

Modern Light Bulb
20,000 hours

Because of the brain-melting scale of a few centuries of continuous improvements, a day's labor buys 20,000 times as much light as it did just two hundred years ago. This happened because people figured out lots of clever ways to get more output for each hour of work. Not just light; we can now produce profoundly more food and clothes and everything else than our grandparents could. We work less and get more.

This productivity growth isn't all good. The environmental consequences have been devastating.

But it has made almost everyone richer. It means, in real terms, almost everybody has more money than their ancestors could have imagined.

CHAPTER 9

But Really: *Can* Everybody Have More Money?

When you replace oil lamps with lightbulbs, people don't have to live in the dark anymore. When you build machines that make it cheaper to spin fiber into yarn, people can suddenly afford more than one shirt, more than one dress. But for the guy whose job used to be going around town lighting up each gas-powered streetlight, or the lady whose job used to be spinning yarn in her cottage, those innovations are a disaster.

We celebrate people who create jobs, but in the long run, we get richer by destroying jobs—by figuring out how to do the same amount of work with fewer people. This is not quite a paradox (because there's an eventual solution to the problem, which we'll get to). But for the people caught up in the destruction, it sucks.

We live in a moment when this tension is acute—when, as the venture capitalist Marc Andreessen said, software is eating the world. Kayak and Expedia made it easier and cheaper for people to buy plane tickets—by putting travel agents out of business. Trucks driven by computers instead of people will make it cheaper to move goods around the country. As a result, it will be cheaper for us to buy stuff. So we'll be able to buy more stuff, or to buy the same amount of stuff and save more money. Driverless trucks will make us richer as a society. But they will not improve life for truck drivers.

All this has happened before. Maybe not *all* of this. Not the part about the computers, and driverless trucks, and travel agents. But the part about machines taking people's jobs and causing massive upheaval—that part happened very dramatically in the early 1800s in England. And the parallels between what happened then and what's happening now are really striking. Last time, for a long time, it did not go well. Just ask the Luddites.

Sympathy for the Luddites

The story of the original Luddites is way more revelatory than the contemporary meaning of the word suggests. The Luddites weren't people opposed to new technology because they hated change; they were skilled workers who saw machines taking their jobs and decided to fight back.

It happened in England in the early 1800s—in the middle of the Industrial Revolution, which was built on the cloth business. At the time, cloth was really expensive and hard to make; most people could only afford one or two sets of clothes. Cloth making required many specialized steps and was mostly done by skilled artisans who worked at home or in small shops. Women would take raw wool or cotton and spin it into yarn. Men would weave it into rough cloth on a hand loom. And then these other guys called croppers would crop the fuzz of the cloth with giant, forty-pound shears.

Many of the people who could make cloth were making a good living by the standards of the time, and they had the freedom of working for themselves. Weavers would walk into the pub with a five-pound note stuck in their hat—conspicuous consumption, a hundred years before the term was coined. Artisans even had a tradition called "St. Monday," which was basically getting really drunk on Sunday, then taking Monday off.

The fact that the jobs paid well was part of their undoing. If you're a worker, getting paid a lot for your work is great. But if you are the cloth merchant paying all these spinners and weavers and croppers, at some point, you start thinking, there's got to be a cheaper way to do this. And at this moment in England, people were starting to build new machines that did all these different things. Someone invented a machine to spin fiber into yarn. Someone else came up with a machine that could turn that yarn into cloth with fewer workers. Another inventor figured out a way to trim the fuzz off fabric so you didn't need the croppers and their forty-pound scissors.

Sort of like in Silicon Valley today, there was all this action. People were getting rich, people were making deals. One example: stockings. Stockings were big back then. (Picture in your mind a portrait of the Founding Fathers, then zoom in on their calves. Stockings.) According to local lore, a "workman named Roper" in rural England built a "rude and imperfect" prototype of a machine that could make ribbed stockings. Then a local farmer who wanted to get into the stocking game sold a horse for £5 and used the money to buy the rights to the machine from Roper. The farmer died a rich man; no sources tell us how Roper felt about the deal.

This is really the first time in history that technological change for workers happened on this scale and at this rate. Today, we assume change is constant, and that some jobs—blacksmiths, switchboard operators, travel agents—will just disappear. But back then, the world wasn't like that. Things didn't change that much from one generation to the next. In earlier times, British law had actually restricted new machines that threatened workers. Allowing these new machines at that time was a choice that the British government was making. To the skilled workers of the day, it seemed like a bad choice.

The cloth workers thought they could convince the country to make a different choice by launching a kind of underground war against the machines. In 1811, mysterious letters started showing up in newspapers and on the walls of village markets and in the mailboxes of the owners of the machines. Here's one. (Shearing frames, by the way, are machines that replaced the croppers with giant shears.)

To Mr Smith Shearing Frame Holder at Hill End Yorkshire.

Sir

Information has just been given in that you are a holder of those detestable Shearing Frames, and I was desired by my Men to write to you and give you fair Warning to pull them down ... if they are not taken down by the end of next Week, I will detach one of my Lieutenants with at least 300 Men to destroy them and furthermore take Notice that if you give us the Trouble of coming so far we will increase your misfortune by burning your Buildings down to Ashes and if you have Impudence to fire upon any of my Men, they have orders to murder you, & burn all your Housing ...

Signed by the General of the Army of
Redressers
Ned Ludd ...

Edward "Ned" Ludd, rebel leader, founder of the Luddites, was said to be holed up in Sherwood Forest, in Nottinghamshire, like Robin Hood. But also like Robin Hood, Ned Ludd was a myth. There may have been a stocking knitter of that name a few decades before who got mad and smashed up some stocking-making equipment. That's what one newspaper editor said, anyway. But General Ludd, leader of the army of redressers, was an invention—someone made him up, and the myth spread.

People had been writing angry letters before, even occasionally attacking factories. But somehow, appointing a nonexistent general changed things. The invention of Ned Ludd made the whole thing seem bigger. There weren't just a few disgruntled workers. There was a secret army of what people started calling Luddites spreading across northern England.

These Luddites weren't some anti-technology cult. They weren't back-to-the-land proto-hippies. They just wanted to get rid of the machines that were taking their jobs. In Nottinghamshire, in the spring of 1811, they started doing it by force. Almost every night, week after week, a band of armed stocking-frame knitters went out and, using hatchets and sledgehammers, broke into factories and smashed the wooden machines that were being used to knit stockings.

Within a few months Ned Ludd was everywhere. When one factory owner walked down the street, kids taunted him. "I'm Ned Ludd!" "No, I'm Ned Ludd!" One government official got a letter from someone claiming to be Ned Ludd's solicitor filing charges against him in Ludd Court. People sang about Ludd in pubs.

Chant no more your old rhymes about bold Robin Hood

His feats I but little admire

I will sing the Achievements of General Ludd

Now the Hero of Nottinghamshire.

Ludd burned down a cotton weaving factory and attacked machines used to crop wool. There were dozens and dozens of attacks, and they were spreading.

It was only a few decades since the revolution in France, and the authorities in Britain were terrified. In 1812, Parliament introduced a bill to make destroying machines punishable by death. Lord Byron, the poet, had a lesser-known career as a member of Parliament. His very first speech there was in response to the bill. The acts of the Luddites, Byron said,

> ...have arisen from circumstances of the most unparalleled distress.... nothing but absolute want could have driven a large and once honest and industrious body of the people into the commission of excesses so hazardous to themselves, their families, and the community....
>
> These men were willing to dig, but the spade was in other hands; they were not ashamed to beg, but there was none to relieve them. Their own means of subsistence were cut off; all other employments preoccupied; and their excesses, however to be deplored and condemned, can hardly be the subject of surprise....
>
> Setting aside the palpable injustice and the certain inefficiency of the bill, are there not capital punishments sufficient on your statutes? Is there not blood enough upon your penal code that more must be poured forth to ascend to heaven and testify against you? ...Are these the remedies for a starving and desperate populace?

Yes, the Lords decided. Death by hanging was the remedy for a starving and desperate populace. The bill was rushed through Parliament as an emergency measure. But the attacks just kept getting bigger.

On the night of April 11, about a hundred Luddites gathered in a field near a town called Huddersfield in the north of England. Many of them were croppers—the guys with the heavy shears who trimmed the fuzz off woolen cloth—and they were there to attack a factory on the edge of town. More people joined them as they walked to the factory; eventually, there were about 150 people in all. They had whatever weapons they could find—guns, hammers, hatchets. Some just had stones. They weren't going after the factory owner, William Cartwright. They were going to destroy his machines—the machines that were stealing their jobs.

Cartwright had just started using shearing frames, the machines that were replacing the croppers. The month before, Luddites had destroyed a wagonload of new machines bound for Cartwright's factory, and he was prepared for a direct attack.

He had started sleeping in the factory, along with four soldiers and five of his workmen. The soldiers were stationed upstairs, where they could crouch behind stone defenses and shoot out at attackers. Cartwright reinforced the factory door with iron studs and bars. He put a vat of sulfuric acid at the top of the stairs, to pour down on attackers who made it through the door. A gate outside the factory yard was patrolled by two sentries.

Just after midnight, the Luddites marched on the factory. They managed to capture the sentries, and they broke through the gate with hatchets. Inside the factory, a dog started barking. Cartwright woke up and roused the guards, who started shooting from the second story. The Luddites with sledgehammers and hatchets tried to break down the door, but they couldn't get through it. They retreated, then attacked again. They shot out the windows but didn't hit anybody inside. Two Luddites were shot dead by the guards.

Eventually, the Luddites retreated. The battle was over; the Luddites lost.

Hundreds of people attended the funeral of one of the dead Luddites. (The other was buried in secret to prevent public mourning.) More troops were sent to the area, but for a long time no trial resulted. For months, nobody would say who was at the attack on the mill. In other towns, attacks continued. One mill owner who had said he wanted to "ride up to his saddle girths in Luddite blood" was shot dead in the street.

Eventually, the government started making arrests. About sixty Luddites were thrown into a castle's jail. There was a quick trial, and fourteen Luddites were sentenced to death, including eight of the men who had attacked Cartwright's mill. The scaffold was built twice as high as usual so more people could see the condemned Luddites hang.

Ned Ludd popped up here and there for a little while longer. But that was basically the end of the Luddites. The last we hear from them is in a brief apocalyptic letter in 1817, suggesting a big, climactic finish was at hand: "The last die will be cast and either the Luddites or the military will have the Command."

There was no big, climactic finish. The military had the command. The Luddites disappeared. Within a few decades, nobody spun or wove or cropped cloth by hand anymore. That world where cloth workers had St. Mondays and five-pound notes in their hats at the pub was gone.

It's tempting to shout back across history to the Luddites: "Trust me. The machines are going to make things so much better. Your descendants will have enough to eat, and shoes on their feet, and they'll be able to take vacations and won't even have to work much until they're eighteen years old. Everyone will get richer. Everyone will have more money."

But for the Luddites, things didn't get better. Things didn't even get better for their kids. For the whole first half of the nineteenth century, as England was building the first modern industrial economy on the planet, and productivity was going through the roof, average wages for workers barely budged. Factory owners got rich. Workers who were good at building factories or repairing machines did pretty well. But it was a bad time to be a skilled artisan whose job could be done by a machine. The Luddites who destroyed machines were not deluded. They didn't have the right to vote or to form unions, so they pursued their economic self-interest by destroying machines. One historian called it "collective bargaining by riot."

We are living in the middle of a second machine age. It's computers and software now, not weaving machines. But some of the same things are happening. People talk about the rise of the 1 percent. About how income for ordinary people is stagnant. Part of that is caused by technological change.

The traditional economist's response to this is: these problems are temporary. Technology means everyone can have more money in the long run. But one thing the Luddites have to teach us is the long run can be really, really long.

IV

MODERN MONEY

The world where productivity took off and the Luddites got hosed was also the world where the international gold standard was born. This was not a coincidence.

The world we live in today—the world where money is issued by governments and backed by nothing—was born when the gold standard nearly destroyed the global economy. This is also not a coincidence.

CHAPTER 10

The Gold Standard: A Love Story

Gold is an atom. It has 79 protons. It's created when neutron stars collide. It existed for billions of years before the first person was born, and it will continue to exist for billions of years after the last person is dead. Gold is not a fiction, it isn't subjective, and it isn't some made-up thing.

This is the dream of gold as money: natural, objective, eternal money, money without human foolishness, money without government. In the nineteenth century, when belief in free markets spread across the Western world, politicians and bankers and intellectuals fell in love with the gold standard. They dreamed of gold as money that flowed naturally around the world like water.

It did not end well.

Start with David Hume, the eighteenth-century Scottish skeptic of everything, an atheist at a time when that was a truly shocking thing to be, a philosopher and historian who got a striking number of things about the world right. His toy model of how money worked became etched in the brains of the people who ran the world and loved the gold standard. Hume was known as the Great Infidel for his religious views, but he created an orthodoxy of money that lasted for generations.

Here's how countries thought about money and wealth when Hume came on the scene: gold (and silver) are wealth. So if we want our nation to be wealthy, we should pile up as much gold as we can. The way to do this is to run a trade surplus—sell more stuff to other countries than they sell to us. That way, more gold will come into the country than will leave it. Our pile of money will get bigger. We'll be richer. To make this happen, we should limit imports (quotas) or put high taxes on them (tariffs). If this argument sounds familiar, it's because it's the way some contemporary politicians talk about trade.

This, Hume said, was all wrong.

Hume used a thought experiment to make his case. Say four-fifths of the gold and silver in Great Britain disappeared overnight. Poof! What happens next? Farmers keep growing wheat. Workers keep weaving cloth and digging coal. And now, because gold and silver are scarcer, each piece of gold and silver—each coin—becomes four times as valuable. If it used to take four pieces of silver to buy a bushel of wheat or to pay a week's wages, now it only takes one piece of silver.

Within Britain, nothing has really changed in relative terms— a week's wages can still buy a bushel of wheat. In the rest of the world, though, stuff from England suddenly seems super cheap. The Spanish and the French rush to buy British wheat. Now wheat is flowing out of Britain and silver is piling up. "In how little time," Hume wrote, "must this bring back the money, which we had lost, and raise us to the level of all the neighbouring nations?"

The converse is also true. If the amount of gold and silver in Britain suddenly quadrupled, prices would rise. British consumers would rush to buy cheaper goods from France and Spain. The gold and silver would flow back out of Britain.

Whatever happens, prices and trade fall back into balance automatically in what Hume called "the common course of nature." Trying to pile up silver and gold in one country, Hume said, is as silly as trying to make one side of the ocean higher than the other. "All water, wherever it communicates, remains always at a level."

Instead of trying to hoard gold, Hume said, countries should create the conditions for people to do good work and create things of value. Tariffs and quotas, Hume wrote, "serve to no purpose but to check industry, and rob ourselves and our neighbors of the common benefits of art and nature."

Hume published this argument in a book called *Political Discourses*. It was wildly popular. Also, not trivially, Hume seems to have influenced his best friend, Adam Smith, who called Hume's work on money and trade "ingenious." In 1776, Smith published *An Inquiry Into the Nature and Causes of the Wealth of Nations*. It was the birth of modern economics. Also, it was a pretty Humey book. A nation doesn't get wealthy by piling on tariffs to "increase...the quantity of gold and silver," Smith wrote. "In every country it always is and must be the interest of the great body of the people to buy whatever they want of those who sell it cheapest."

Smith's argument in favor of free trade is exactly what the merchants and bankers who were getting rich from trade wanted to hear. In the decades after Smith wrote, they pushed Britain to lower or eliminate many of its tariffs, to stop trying to pile up gold and silver.

Around the same time, Britain made another key change that would help Smith's free-trade views take over much of the world, and that would give Hume's ideas about money more weight than ever. Parliament changed the definition of money and, without really meaning to, created the international gold standard.

The Case Against Gold

Britain, like many countries, tried for a long time to create a currency based on both gold and silver. And, like many countries, it never could set the values right for gold and silver coins. In Britain's case, the official value of silver coins was lower than their value as raw metal, so, as in John Law's day, people kept melting down silver coins into lumps of silver and selling the lumps in Europe as scrap metal.

In 1816, Parliament gave up. They declared that the British pound sterling would henceforth be defined as 123 grains of gold, and nothing else. (The grain is an ancient unit of weight based on a grain of wheat; there are 480 grains in a troy ounce.) No one knew it yet, but the era of the international gold standard had begun.

Britain had the most important economy in the world at the time, and London was the center of the financial universe. Lots of countries had long struggled to figure out the right ratio between gold and silver for their money. So, one by one, other countries abandoned silver. By the late 1800s, every major economy in the world was effectively on the gold standard. In the United States, year in and year out, $20.67 got you an ounce of gold, and an ounce of gold got you $20.67. It was as basic, and as constant, as saying an hour is equal to sixty minutes, and sixty minutes are equal to an hour.

Having every major economy in the world on the gold standard solved lots of economic problems. It made international trade easier. Because every country's currency was always convertible to gold at the same rate, the relative value of different currencies stayed the same. ($4.87 bought you £1, always.) In essence the international gold standard was like having a single international currency. Along with new technologies like steamships and railroads and the telegraph, the gold standard helped propel the first great wave of globalization. People in countries like the United States and Argentina got richer by selling stuff to Europe, and people in Europe got richer by investing in countries like the United States and Argentina. In Britain especially, tariffs came down. Gold flowed back and forth like water. Smith's and Hume's dreams had come true. What could possibly go wrong?

*　*　*

In the second half of the nineteenth century, as one country after another joined the international gold standard, the world's economy grew faster than the world's gold supply. The amount of stuff people wanted to buy grew faster than the amount of gold available to buy stuff. As a result, demand for gold increased, and gold got more expensive. Under the gold standard, when gold gets more expensive, the price of everything else falls.

In Hume's thought experiment, where gold disappears overnight and the price of everything falls, nothing really changes domestically because relative prices stay the same. Workers' wages fall just the same amount as the price of goods, so everybody can buy the same amount of stuff. But Hume, in his too-beautiful-to-live thought experiment, largely left out an essential function of money: debt.

If I borrow $1,000 today, and tomorrow my paycheck and the price of everything I buy gets cut in half, I am screwed. Now I have to work twice as long to make my monthly debt payments! On the other hand, if I'm not in debt, and I have $1,000 in the bank when prices fall, I'm psyched: I can now buy twice as much stuff as I could yesterday. Deflation is bad for debtors and good for creditors.

After the United States shifted from a gold-and-silver standard to a gold standard in 1873, prices fell for twenty years. This was very good for rich people, whose money bought more and more stuff. It was very bad for poor people who owed money and had to keep working more and more just to make the same monthly payments. As a result, a fight broke out over what should count as money in America.

Farmers, who often borrow money to buy land, were getting screwed by the gold standard and the falling prices that came with it. Some supported the Greenback Party, which called for the government to print (green) paper money not backed by precious metal, as it had briefly done during the Civil War. But this was a radical position (paper that couldn't be exchanged for gold or silver still seemed ridiculous) and never really took off.

So the farmers started arguing for the United States to go back to the way things used to be, when the government stood ready to trade money for either gold or silver. In that world, anybody could bring raw silver or gold to the US Mint and get coins in return. Adding silver back into the mix would mean quite simply that there was more money. This would make prices rise, which would make it easier for farmers to make their debt payments.

Here is a thing that always happens with money: whatever money is at a given moment comes to seem like the natural form money should take, and anything else seems like irresponsible craziness. This myopia peaked with the gold standard. After twenty years on the gold standard, people had already come to believe that the gold standard was obviously the only natural way to do money. Every civilized country does it. Who would ever consider doing money differently?

By the 1890s, almost all Republicans and most Democrats

agreed that the United States should stay on the gold standard, and the pleas of farmers fell largely on deaf ears.

That changed—at least for Democrats—on July 9, 1896, when the party met in Chicago to choose a candidate for president. Late that morning, a thirty-six-year-old former congressman named William Jennings Bryan rose from his seat and walked up to the stage. He was about to give the most famous speech in presidential campaign history and launch a campaign centered on the meaning of money.

Bryan was known as an orator—he traveled around the country getting paid to speak—and he looked the part. "His stalwart, broad-shouldered presence fills and satisfies the eye," one newspaper wrote. "His face, with its black eyebrows and strong features, shows the expression afar off." One other thing about Bryan, which was not trivial given that he was going to be speaking to 20,000 people in an arena bigger than a football field, without using a microphone: he was really loud. His wife once said she was sitting inside a hotel room and could hear her husband perfectly. He was speaking three blocks away.

That day in Chicago, facing a divided party, Bryan began speaking directly to those in the audience on the other side: the Democrats who wanted to keep America on gold.

When you come before us and tell us that we shall disturb your business interests, we reply that you have disturbed our business interests by your action. We say to you that you have made too limited in its application the definition of a businessman. The man who is employed for wages is as much a businessman as his employer.... The farmer who goes forth in the morning and toils all day...is as much a businessman as the man who goes upon the Board of Trade and bets upon the price of grain. The miners who go 1,000 feet into the earth ... and bring forth from their hiding places the precious metals ... are as much businessmen as the few financial magnates who in a backroom corner the money of the world. We come to speak for this broader class of businessmen.

In his memoirs, Bryan said this idea that the gold standard is actually bad for business—if you define business broadly—was the most important argument of the speech. But nobody remembers that part of the speech, because the speech wasn't really an argument. It was a cross between a declaration of war and a sermon. And as he shifted roles from political debater to bellicose preacher, Bryan switched audiences. He stopped trying to convince the advocates of the gold standard and started rallying the silverites.

We are fighting in the defense of our homes, our families, and posterity. We have petitioned, and our petitions have been scorned. We have entreated, and our entreaties have been disregarded. We have begged, and they have mocked when our calamity came. We beg no longer; we entreat no more; we petition no more. We defy them! ...

If they dare to come out in the open field and defend the gold standard as a good thing, we shall fight them to the uttermost, having behind us the producing masses of the nation and the world. ... we shall answer their demands for a gold standard by saying to them, you shall not press down upon the brow of labor this crown of thorns. You shall not crucify mankind upon a cross of gold!

As he spoke that last line, Bryan stepped back from the podium, stretched his arms out as if he were on the cross, and stood there, silently, for several seconds. It was a bold move, and it wasn't clear how it would play to the room.

Very well, it turned out. As Bryan walked down from the stage and into the crowd, one reporter wrote, "Everybody seemed to go mad at once." People shouted and waved umbrellas and threw their hats across the room. Two bands started playing two different songs. Old men wept. A farmer banged on his chair and yelled, "My God! My God! My God!" The crowd lifted Bryan on their shoulders and carried him around the room. Delegations from dozens of southern and western states rushed with their banners to stand next to Bryan's Nebraska delegation. The next day, they elected Bryan the Democratic nominee for president.

William McKinley was not impressed. McKinley was the Republican nominee, and his shtick that year was giving speeches from the front porch of his house in Ohio. The day after Bryan's nomination, two days after the "cross of gold" speech, McKinley stood up on a chair on his porch and gave his own speech to a group of Republicans who had come to see him:

> My fellow citizens, recent events have imposed upon the patriotic people of this country a responsibility and a duty greater than that of any since the Civil War. Then it was a struggle to preserve the government of the United States. Now it is a struggle to preserve the financial honor of the government . . .
>
> Our creed embraces an honest dollar, an untarnished national credit . . . Upon this platform we stand, and submit its declarations to the sober and considerate judgment of the American people.

Like Bryan, McKinley was selling morality more than any particular economic argument. But instead of Bryan's morality of oppression (by gold) and salvation (through silver), McKinley's was the morality of "responsibility," "duty," and "honor." Anyone of "sober and considerate judgement" would favor the "honest dollar" of gold—as opposed, implicitly, to the dishonest dollar of silver.

If the gold standard caused falling prices and hurt borrowers, the moral logic went, it was good for savers—it made their money more valuable. It rewarded virtuous thrift and punished the slackers who lived beyond their means and had to borrow to get by.

Everybody remembers Bryan's "cross of gold" speech. Nobody remembers McKinley's "sober and considerate judgement" speech. But somehow Bryan lost the election and McKinley won. Americans voted for McKinley's buttoned-up America of anxiety and success, not Bryan's biblical America of terror and deliverance.

That year, there were new gold discoveries in the Klondike. Around the same time, people were figuring out better ways of extracting gold from ore. Now the supply of gold was growing faster than the world economy, and prices started rising. Under the gold standard, the world's supply of the basic form of money is driven not by economic needs or political demands. It's just, how much gold do miners happen to be pulling out of the ground this year? If it's a lot, there will be a lot more money, and prices will rise. If it's a little, prices will fall. It's a weird way to run a currency.

In 1900, McKinley signed the Gold Standard Act, which formalized what had been effectively true for a generation: America was a gold-standard nation. When McKinley ran for reelection that year (again against Bryan), one of his campaign posters showed a drawing of McKinley standing on a gold coin, with the words "commerce" and "civilization" written next to him. Subtle! McKinley—and the gold standard—won again.

The Money Illusion

Irving Fisher was a Yale economist, a health-food zealot, a prohibitionist, and a fitness guru who filled a floor of his New Haven mansion with exercise equipment. He coauthored a book called *How to Live: Rules for Healthful Living Based on Modern Science*, which sold half a million copies, the royalties of which Fisher gave to an organization he'd founded called the Life Extension Institute.

He invented a card filing system to organize all his projects, then patented it, then created a company called Index Visible to sell the card system, then merged his company with a bigger company and made a fortune. Fisher was a proponent of eugenics, which was widely popular at the time but is today clearly repulsive and immoral. At various times he also proposed a thirteen-month calendar, a simplified spelling system, and a new system for making maps. All of which is to say he was not only someone who wanted to understand the world but also to change it.

In the 1896 presidential campaign, Fisher was a young professor and, like pretty much every economist in America, he campaigned against Bryan. He shared the moral indignation of the pro-gold crew, but he also had a more intellectually rigorous reason to believe in the gold standard.

The month after Bryan was nominated, Fisher published a book called *Appreciation and Interest*. He argued that when people expect prices to rise, lenders demand higher interest rates to compensate; when people expect prices to fall, interest rates go down. (So, for example, if I want to lend you money for a year at 5 percent interest, and I think inflation is going to be 2 percent, I'll charge 7 percent interest. If I think prices are going to fall by 1 percent, I'll charge 4 percent interest.)

As a result, the real interest people pay—the interest after accounting for expected inflation or deflation—doesn't change with rising or falling prices. In other words, Fisher suggested, steadily falling prices under the gold standard didn't really matter. All those farmers who were complaining about their debts would have been paying higher interest rates if prices were rising instead of falling. In the end, the amount they had to work to pay their debts would have been the same whether or not silver was money.

But in the years that followed, Fisher looked more closely at the data. Then he did something that famous economists (or, for that matter, people in general) almost never do: he admitted he was wrong.

Fisher saw that in the real world, unlike in his models, interest rates don't go up and down in lockstep with expected inflation and deflation. As he later wrote, in 1896 he "had not come to appreciate the evils of unstable money, nor how impossible it was for business men to provide against them through foresight alone."

Fisher became obsessed with the way changes in the value of the dollar could mess up people's lives, and with figuring out ways to solve the problem. At his index-card company, he put his economic theories to work by tying employees' wages to inflation and deflation. When prices went up, pay went up; when prices went down, pay went down. Employees' inflation-adjusted pay stayed the same. (Raises were handled separately.) So rational!

"As long as the cost of living was getting higher, the Index Visible employees welcomed the swelling contents of their 'high Cost of Living' pay envelopes," Fisher wrote. "They thought their wages were increasing, though it was carefully explained to them that their real wages were merely standing still. But as soon as the cost of living fell they resented the 'reduction' in wages."

Fisher wrote a book called *The Money Illusion* about this kind of thinking error. We think a dollar today is the same as a dollar a year ago. It's not; that's the illusion.

If I bought a house for $100,000 in 1975 and sold it for $400,000 in 2020, it may have felt like a windfall, but I actually lost money on the deal—$400,000 in 2020 bought less than $100,000 in 1975.

The movie with the biggest US box-office gross wasn't *Star Wars: The Force Awakens*, which brought in over $900 million in 2015 and 2016, but *Gone With the Wind*, which brought in $200 million in 1939 (because $200 million in 1939 bought far more than $900 million in 2016).

If I get a pay cut of 1 percent, and prices fall by 2 percent, I'm actually getting a raise. My new salary buys more stuff than my old salary.

But of course nobody thinks this way.

The money illusion was especially strong under the gold standard. Indeed, the gold standard, in a way, was built on the money illusion. The whole point of the gold standard was that the value of a dollar didn't change, right? A dollar was the same amount of gold, year in and year out. This argument made Fisher crazy.

"Our dollar is now simply a fixed weight of gold—a unit of weight, masquerading as a unit of value.... What good does it do us to be assured that our dollar *weighs* just as much as ever? Does this fact help us in the least to bear the high cost of living? What we really want to know is whether the dollar *buys* as much as ever."

"We tenaciously cling to the blissful assumption that our dollar never varies," Fisher wrote. "We seem to like not only, as Barnum said, to be humbugged, but to humbug ourselves."

Even when people saw through the money illusion, Fisher realized, the dollar was subject to swings in value that no one could predict.

These unexpected swings, when prices rose or fell across the board, arbitrarily shifted huge sums of money between lenders and borrowers. This wasn't only unfair; it was terrible for the economy. Any perfectly good business—the best-run farm, the most honest bank, the most efficient factory—could go bust just by getting unlucky and falling on the wrong side of inflation or deflation. To Fisher, a dollar that varied unpredictably in value from year to year was as absurd and as outdated as a minute that varied in length from year to year.

The solution, Fisher thought, was obvious: redefine the meaning of money. Instead of defining the dollar as a fixed amount of gold, define it as a fixed basket of stuff. "We want a dollar which will always buy the same aggregate quantity of bread, butter, beef, bacon, beans, sugar, clothing, fuel, and the other essential things for which we spend it," he wrote. Fisher's idea was brilliant—and very close to the way the dollar works today.

But getting from the gold dollar to Fisher's new, stable dollar was tricky. As he wrote much later, if he had just come out and suggested cutting the dollar's link to gold, he "would have been hooted down." So Fisher proposed an overly complicated, impossible-to-execute idea that involved frequently changing the gold content of the dollar so that the price of everything else would stay the same. If prices rose, the government would redefine the dollar to be worth a little less gold. That would bring prices back down. And vice versa. It was a sort of pretend gold standard.

Fisher being Fisher, he pitched this idea everywhere he could. Also, Fisher being Fisher, he kept track of all the pitching: "99 addresses, besides 37 letters to the press, and 161 special articles, as well as 9 testimonies at hearings held by government bodies and 12 privately printed circulars, together with 13 books bearing on the subject." He created a "Stable Money League" to push for his policies, and on New Year's Eve of 1920, Fisher and a few other stable-money true believers went to the Washington Monument, where, he wrote, "we ushered in the New Year by dedicating ourselves to the new movement."

At the time, people didn't talk about inflation the way we do today. They talked about the high cost of living, but usually in a vague, qualitative way. They thought of the prices of particular goods increasing, but not of some aggregate, quantifiable price level. So Fisher spent years analyzing different methods for calculating price indexes. He even started a company to sell the index numbers to newspapers, which started printing them every week.

And he made a genius propaganda move. Fisher knew people thought the dollar was stable and prices varied; he wanted to convince them that widespread price changes meant the value of the dollar itself was changing. So instead of publishing a "price index," he published a "purchasing power of money" index. Rather than saying "prices rose last week," Fisher's index said "the purchasing power of the dollar fell." Mathematically, it's just another way of saying the same thing. But the shift was essential.

"I had come to realize that people could not get interested in stabilizing the dollar until they saw that it was unstable," Fisher wrote. "The index of the dollar's purchasing power gave to several million people every Monday morning the opportunity to read of the weekly change in the dollar." If he wanted to win people over to his movement, Fisher realized he first had to change the way they thought about money.

In the boom of the 1920s, Fisher sold his index-card company for a fortune, then invested that fortune in the booming stock market and watched it grow. He spent his money on his obsessions, including $20,000 a year on propaganda for stable money, and a full-time salary for a personal trainer and physician. The physician had invented a variation on volleyball that Fisher called "battle ball." Fisher "had a cement court built behind the rose garden, where he ran the...members of his staff ragged at midmorning and midafternoon workouts," his son wrote.

Fisher was a happy warrior. He believed that he and other scientists were figuring out how to solve the world's problems. And he was confident that the new technologies of the day—radio, mass-produced consumer goods—and new, better management justified the booming stock market.

In a speech on October 15, 1929, Fisher said the market had hit "a permanently high plateau." His pronouncement was frozen in carbonite in the next day's *New York Times*: "FISHER SEES STOCKS PERMANENTLY HIGH." Fisher's timing was exquisite. Two weeks later, the market crashed.

To the extent Fisher is remembered today, he is remembered for being spectacularly wrong about the stock market. But he was right about money. The stock market crash of 1929 was (obviously) very bad. But it was not, on its own, enough to cause the Great Depression. What turned the crash into a worldwide disaster was the gold standard and the profound instability that went with it.

To be fair, it wasn't the gold standard alone that broke the world. It was helped along by the powerful institutions that were at the center of money, and that saw themselves as the guardians of the gold standard: central banks. In the United States, that meant the Federal Reserve.

CHAPTER 11

Just Don't Call It a Central Bank

Today, the Federal Reserve is one of the most powerful institutions in the world. It can create trillions of dollars out of thin air, affecting approximately everybody who uses money anywhere on Earth.

But when the stock market crashed in 1929, the Fed was less than twenty years old. It was a weird central bank, which at first nobody even wanted to call a central bank, because America had just spent a hundred years fighting over whether to have a central bank at all.

The story of that fight is the story of figuring out how to do money in a democracy. What should the government do and what should be left to the free market? Who gets to profit and who gets bailed out? And perhaps most fundamentally: Who gets to print money?

The story starts a century before the Fed was founded, when the second most powerful person in America (a banker) went to war with the most powerful person in America (the president) over a central bank that no one quite knew was a central bank.

The banker was Nicholas Biddle. He was a boy genius who grew up in Philadelphia and graduated first in his class at Princeton at age fifteen, in 1801. Like a lot of people who finish college and don't know what to do, he became a lawyer and hated it. He wrote in a letter that he saw his life reduced to "pleading the defenseless cases of vice and misfortune, and then dying like a mushroom on the soil which had seen me grow." As side hustles, he ran a literary magazine and edited the journals of William Clark, of Lewis and Clark fame.

When Biddle was twenty-four, he was elected to the Pennsylvania state legislature. Fighting about banking and money was America's national pastime in the early nineteenth century (baseball hadn't been invented yet), and Biddle jumped into the middle of it.

The idea of the government printing money was so ridiculous as to be out of the question. During the American Revolution, the Continental Congress had printed paper money to pay for the war, and then printed some more, and some more, and soon it had become worth almost nothing. The standard source of paper money was private banks, which were granted charters by state governments. Each bank printed its own paper money, redeemable on demand at the bank for silver or gold. Everybody agreed that was okay.

The fight—the endlessly recurring power-and-money-in-America fight—was over whether Congress should allow the creation of a single, national bank. Certainly it would be convenient. The bank could print paper money for people to use across the whole country, and the government could use the bank to easily move money from state to state. But a single, national bank would also be a huge concentration of power in private hands, and there was a debate over whether the Constitution even allowed for a national bank. (James Madison, the father of the Constitution, seemed to go back and forth on the issue.)

Congress created a national bank, then killed it twenty years later, then created a second national bank. It was called, reasonably enough, the Second Bank of the United States. The Second Bank had a bit of a rough start—specifically, a bunch of people who worked for the bank stole money. Also the bank's policies helped cause a massive financial crisis in 1819. That year, President Monroe appointed Nicholas Biddle a director of the bank. Four years later, Biddle's fellow directors picked him to be the bank's president.

It's tough to overstate how powerful the president of the bank was. Imagine if, today, the Chairman of the Federal Reserve was also the CEO of JPMorgan Chase—and JPMorgan Chase was bigger than Apple, Google, and ExxonMobil combined. Being president of the Second Bank of the United States was sort of like that. It was the second most powerful job in America. Fortunately for America, Biddle was really good at the job.

By the time Biddle became president of the bank, there were around 250 state banks scattered around the country. All of them made loans and issued their own paper money. Like banks in all times, these banks sometimes got out of control—they started lending more and more money to riskier and riskier borrowers. When a bank loaned out too much money or suddenly saw a bunch of loans go bad, it might find itself unable to redeem its paper money for gold. This was, of course, bad for the people who held the paper money, but it was bad for the local economy more generally. When the value of a dollar became unclear, when credit froze up, it became much harder to do business.

Biddle guided the Second Bank of the United States into a new role. It became a regulator of the state banks, and of the banking system more generally, to try to prevent these violent swings in lending by the state banks. He told Congress he saw it as the Bank's duty "to keep the State banks within proper limits; to make them shape their business according to their means."

The government still accepted state banknotes in payment for things like customs duties and land purchases (there was no income tax at the time). As part of its role as banker to the federal government, the Bank allowed people to make those payments at its branches. Accumulating state banknotes gave the Bank power to rein in any state bank by turning in the notes and demanding that the bank pay out gold or silver, or sign over loans the banks had issued.

Biddle also used the Bank to buffer swings in international trade, accumulating gold when it flowed into the country, and dispersing it to state banks at moments when gold was rushing out of the country and becoming harder for the banks to come by.

He was unambiguously successful. People came to trust banks more, the United States finally had an integrated financial system, and the era was both prosperous and stable.

The idea that you should use a bank to regulate other banks, and indeed to regulate the flow of money itself throughout an economy, is obvious today. The United States and every other major country have central banks to do exactly that. But the idea isn't obvious in the abstract, and it wasn't obvious in the 1820s. The Bank of England had existed for more than one hundred years, but people were still arguing over what its responsibilities were. Was it just a private bank? Did it have some duty to the nation?

The term "central bank" didn't even exist yet, but Biddle was ahead of his time. One modern financial historian called Biddle "the world's first self-conscious central banker"—the first person to run a central bank with a belief that his responsibilities weren't just to his shareholders' money, but to the nation's money.

The President Who Hated Banks

In 1828, when Biddle was at the peak of his powers, Andrew Jackson was elected president. Jackson was the opposite of Nicholas Biddle.

Jackson went off to fight in the Revolutionary War at age thirteen, was an orphan at fifteen, and grew up to become a frontiersman and a general. Biddle edited a literary magazine; Jackson killed a man in a duel. Biddle got famous for making a speech; Jackson got famous for defeating the British in the Battle of New Orleans in the War of 1812. Biddle edited the journals of Lewis and Clark; Jackson was famous in his lifetime and is notorious today for his slaughter of Native Americans. Biddle learned to control the nation's paper money; Jackson learned to hate paper money.

By the time Jackson was eighteen he owned land in Tennessee and was running a store with his brother-in-law. On a business trip to Philadelphia, he sold some land on credit to a merchant, then used that credit to buy stuff for the store (roughly equivalent to taking a personal check from the merchant, then endorsing it over to buy the stuff). The merchant wasn't good for the money, and Jackson wound up on the hook. He had to sell the store to pay off the creditors. After that, Jackson didn't like debt, or banks, or paper money. He thought money was silver and gold coins, and everything else was a scheme cooked up by bankers to rip people off.

Jackson was elected president in 1828. In 1829, when Biddle paid a courtesy call to the White House, Jackson told him, "I do not dislike your bank any more than all banks."

This may have been a lie. Jackson's general vibe was that he was a man of the people, opposed to East Coast elites and wary of federal power. The Bank of the United States was all of that rolled into one:

the federal government granting special privileges to rich bankers who used those privileges to get even richer. To Jackson, it was obvious that such a massive concentration of power in a private company was undemocratic—"dangerous to our liberties," in his words.

At the time, companies were created by special permission of lawmakers and were given finite charters; if lawmakers didn't like a company, they could kill it by letting the charter expire. The Bank of the United States had a twenty-year charter that was set to expire in 1836. Biddle wanted to get the charter renewed before Jackson got reelected; Congress sided with Biddle and passed a bill to recharter the Bank. Biddle showed up on the floor of the House, then threw a party nearby to celebrate.

"They feasted high and drank toasts and made speeches, and celebrated the victory," Jackson's attorney general, Roger Taney, wrote later, "taking pains to make their rejoicing sufficiently vociferous to be heard in the streets and sufficiently public to make sure that it would reach the ears of the President. And after enjoying his triumph Mr. Biddle left Washington without deigning to pay the President the ordinary visit of etiquette. It was treated as his victory: or rather the certain harbinger of Genl. Jackson's overthrow." In other words, in Taney's telling, that party was Biddle's screw you to Jackson.

Jackson was a brawler, and his response was typical. After the party, he said to his vice president: "The bank, Mr. Van Buren, is trying to kill me. But I will kill it."

A few days later Jackson vetoed the bill. He had enough support in Congress to sustain the veto: the Bank's charter would not be renewed. Jackson won; Biddle lost. The United States wouldn't have a central bank for more than seventy years.

When the charter of the Bank of the United States expired, Biddle got a charter from the Pennsylvania legislature and turned the bank into the United States Bank of Pennsylvania (the "of Pennsylvania" reads like a sad-trombone punchline). He dreamed briefly of making a comeback—of getting a new, national charter. Instead, the bank went bankrupt in 1841. Biddle died three years later, despondent.

When Jackson had vetoed the Bank's recharter, back in 1832, he had delivered the news to Congress with a high-minded veto message, written partly by Taney, his attorney general. The message attacked the Bank as a dangerous concentration of power in private hands. This was a reasonable argument! It *was* a profound concentration of power, and, though Biddle was a good, public-minded banker, his successor might have been a villain.

Jackson also called the Bank a tool of the rich. "It is to be regretted that the rich and powerful too often bend the acts of government to their selfish purposes," the veto message said. "When the laws undertake...to make the rich richer and the potent more powerful, the humble members of society—the farmers, mechanics, and laborers—who have neither the time nor the means of securing like favors to themselves, have a right to complain of the injustice of their Government."

But his veto was not a blow against the rich or against bankers in general. It was a blow against the Bank of the United States and its rich investors—and also a windfall for state banks and their rich investors. Without the Bank of the United States to hold them in check, state banks could now run wild, making more loans and printing more paper money than ever.

A Country with 8,370 Kinds of Money

In many parts of America in the 1840s and '50s, anyone who wanted to could print money. Not surprisingly, lots of people wanted to.

Until this time, if you wanted to create a bank, you had to get special permission from the state legislature. This often meant bribing half the legislators in the state (half plus one if you wanted to be sure to get your charter). Scandals ensued.

So in 1837, just after the Second Bank ceased to be a national bank, when the United States found itself without a national paper currency, states started passing laws that said anyone who followed certain rules could start a bank and print their own banknotes.

The rules said that to print money, a bank had to buy some bonds and deposit them with the state banking regulator. (In a lot of states, these had to be government bonds, but some states let banks use railroad bonds, or even mortgages.) For every dollar of bonds the bank deposited, it could print a dollar of paper money, which it could then lend out to its customers. Anyone could walk into the bank and redeem the paper money for silver or gold coins. If the bank went bust, the state regulator could sell the bonds the bank had deposited and use the proceeds to redeem the paper money the bank had printed.

This was called free banking, and, perhaps unsurprisingly, it didn't always work. Sometimes the bonds fell in value so that, even when they were all sold, there wasn't enough gold and silver to redeem the paper money. And sometimes banks just didn't follow the rules.

States tried to keep banks honest by requiring them to hold a minimum reserve of gold and silver, and sending inspectors around to check on the banks. In Michigan, bankers responded by posting spies on the roads. The spies would alert the local banker when an inspector was coming so the banker could scramble to get some gold before the inspector showed up. "Gold and silver flew about the country with the celerity of magic," an oddly poetic state banking commissioner wrote in 1838. "Its sound was heard in the depths of the forest; yet, like the wind, one knew not whence it came or whither it was going." Some banks showed state inspectors what appeared to be boxes full of gold coins, but were in fact just a thin icing of gold coins on top of a box full of nails.

Not all banks were shady. Not even most banks were shady. But the notes printed by the shady banks looked as legit as the notes printed by the honest banks. And there were a lot of notes—at one point, the *Chicago Tribune* reported that the country had 8,370 different kinds of paper money in circulation. This created a daily absurdity.

A customer walks into a store and asks to buy a sack of flour. The customer hands the storekeeper a random piece of paper with, say, a picture of Santa Claus on it and the name of some bank hundreds of miles away in Waupun, Wisconsin, which sounds (all due respect) like a made-up name for a town. The paper with the picture of Santa Claus says $2. How does the storekeeper know whether to accept it?

He pulls out his *Thompson's Bank Note Reporter*—a handy periodical that lists every bank in America, what the banks' bills look like, and whether the bank is reliably redeeming its money for gold or silver.

The shopkeeper flips to the Wisconsin section, finds Waupun Bank—the bank is legit—and a brief description of the bank's two-dollar bills: "2s, Santa Claus, sleigh reindeers, houses &c." It's real money!

The *Reporter* also tells the storekeeper to apply a 1 percent discount to the note (in other words, to value that $2 bill at $1.98). Discounts varied from city to city—the farther from the issuing bank, the bigger the discount, to account for the cost of returning the bill to the bank for redemption. And, of course, if there were signs that a bank was about to fail, the discount could get very large very quickly.

Thompson also published a counterfeit detector (a world with thousands of different kinds of money is a counterfeiter's dream come true) and a coin supplement that described all the foreign coins that circulated alongside American money.

It was a world where the government set a few rules, then got out of the way—a world where there was a free market in money itself. This was by design. "The people…demanded that the right to deal in money should be as free in its exercise as that of dealing in wheat or in cotton bales," one court wrote, upholding New York's free banking law. It was the world Jackson's cronies had dreamed of.

Here's what a trip from Kentucky to Virginia was like in this world, according to the journals of one traveler:

> Started home with the Kentucky money…at Maysville, wanted Virginia money; couldn't get it. At Wheeling exchanged $50 note, Kentucky money, for notes of the North Western Bank of Virginia; reached Fredericktown; there neither Virginia nor Kentucky money current; paid a $5 Wheeling note for breakfast and dinner; received in change two $1 notes of some Pennsylvania bank, $1 Baltimore and Ohio Railroad and balance in Good Intent shinplasters [worthless paper money];

100 yards from the tavern door all notes refused except the Baltimore and Ohio Railroad.

Finally, our hero writes, he makes it back across the Virginia border—where he has to spend two days negotiating the exchange of his crap money for the Virginia money he needs. He loses 10 percent in the deal.

Free banking sounds like a nightmare—shady banks, all these different pieces of paper with different values, counterfeits, and no central bank to keep the system in check. And clearly sometimes it was a nightmare.

But in the 1970s, as belief in free markets and skepticism of government intervention started to take off, economic historians went back and started to reexamine the free banking era. Rather than rely on anecdotes (like one unlucky traveler's often-cited Kentucky-to-Virginia trip), they tried to look at data—at the total number of banks, the number of bank failures, and how much it typically cost people to change money. And they found that free banking wasn't so bad!

Travelers typically lost around 1 or 2 percent when they exchanged paper money, in the same ballpark as the fee I pay today when I can't get to my bank and have to use another bank's ATM. Also, the historians found, there weren't actually that many shady banks.

And the insane proliferation of paper money issued by the banks across the western frontier had its uses. It meant that settlers could borrow paper money to buy the seed and livestock and equipment they needed to go into business. As the economist John Kenneth Galbraith wrote, "The anarchy served the frontier far better than a more orderly system that kept a tight hand on credit could have done."

When the Civil War broke out and the federal government needed to raise money, Abraham Lincoln's Treasury secretary pushed new laws through Congress that created a kind of free banking for the nation. Now anyone who met certain rules could create a national bank. Crucially, for funding the war, the national banks' paper money had to be backed by US government bonds. In order to exist, national banks had to lend money to the Union. (The Confederacy printed its own money, which became worthless when the South lost the war.)

A final banking bill was signed by President Lincoln on March 3, 1865—"the day before his second inaugural, a month before the fall of Richmond, six weeks before his murder," the economic historian Bray Hammond wrote. The bill put a 10 percent tax on paper money issued by state banks. Its intent was to tax state banknotes out of existence, leaving only the uniform paper money issued by national banks. It worked as intended, and soon all the money printed by state banks was gone.

The Civil War was the moment when people stopped saying "the United States are" and started saying "the United States is"— when it went from being a bunch of different states to being a single country. Destroying the world of thousands of different kinds of money issued by state-chartered banks and creating the world of one kind of paper money—uniform bills issued by national banks— was a small part of that shift. Money is part of what makes a country a country.

Panic Attacks

The paper money printed by the new national banks circulated around the country at face value. So far, so good. But because the money had to be backed by government bonds, the amount of money in circulation was limited by the amount of money the government borrowed. Every fall, when farmers needed money to hire people to harvest their crops, and buyers needed money to buy the crops, there was a shortage of money, and interest rates spiked.

There was another problem, less frequent but more severe, with money in America: massive financial crises. A trigger came every 10 years or so—a big bank would fail, or a speculative bubble would burst—and everybody would rush to turn the money in their bank account into paper money, or to turn their paper money into gold. And, as always, even healthy banks didn't have enough money to withstand a run. The economy would collapse. Millions of people would lose their jobs. Aptly, the crises were called panics.

The Europeans were starting to realize that a central bank—a bank with a government-granted monopoly on printing paper money, and the obligation to manage the nation's money—could make panics less frequent and less severe. The key move was for the central bank to lend money freely to sound borrowers when everybody was panicking.

"They must lend to merchants, to minor bankers, to 'this man and that man,'" Walter Bagehot, a nineteenth-century editor of the *Economist* magazine, famously wrote. If people know that the central bank will lend to keep their bank in business tomorrow, then they won't rush to pull their money out today. And if they don't rush to pull their money out today, there's no panic, no financial crisis.

But America was still living in the shadow of Andrew Jackson. People hated the idea of a central bank, which they figured would be a tool of elites on Wall Street, or elites in Washington, or both, and in any case would rob from the poor and give to the rich and be a general threat to democracy.

Then, in the fall of 1907, a copper magnate who controlled a small New York bank got into financial trouble, and a run on his bank quickly spread to other New York banks. It was the worst financial panic since Andrew Jackson's time. It ended only after J. P. Morgan, the most influential banker in the country, locked a bunch of other bankers in his private library and told them he wouldn't open the door until they agreed on a plan to bail each other out. Then he played solitaire and smoked cigars until they worked it out.

The bankers did come up with a plan, and it did stop the panic, but not in time to save the real economy—unemployment doubled and bankruptcies rose by half. This is what passed for central banking in America in 1907.

Yet the panic didn't convince Americans that they needed a central bank. Instead, one banker wrote, most people were "laying the blame for these difficulties upon the 'selfish and reckless management of corporations,' on 'over-speculation,' the 'greed of banks' or the wily practices of 'Wall Street.'"

Of course banks are greedy! Of course corporations are selfish, and Wall Street is wily! Blaming a financial crisis on these qualities is like blaming a flood on the wetness of water. A twenty-first-century economist pointed out that if Wall Street greed caused financial crises, we'd have a crisis every week. The important question at the time—and, indeed, the question we should always be asking—is: How can we design a monetary system that channels that greed and selfishness and wile toward socially useful ends, and limits the potential harm inherent in finance?

The Panic of 1907 did get some people thinking about these questions—notably a powerful senator named Nelson Aldrich, who was known as the King Pin. He started reading about banking and chaired a monetary commission that went off and toured Europe to see how they did money there.

By 1910, Aldrich was convinced that America needed a central bank, or at least something central bank-ish. But he also knew that Americans wouldn't go for it. So he did what any reasonable senator would do. He gathered a cabal of powerful bankers to go off in secret to plot a central bank that everyone agreed not to call a central bank.

A Senator and a Bunch of Bankers Sneak Off to a Private Island to Plot a Central Bank

On a November night in 1910, a group of prominent men arrived one by one at a private railcar hooked to the back of a train in Hoboken, New Jersey. They included Senator Aldrich, three of the most powerful bankers in America, and a Harvard economist working for the Secretary of the Treasury.

Their trip was a secret. Aldrich had told the men to come alone, in the dark, dressed as duck hunters (complete with rifles), and to use only first names, to conceal their identities. "When I came to that car," one of the bankers wrote decades later, "the blinds were down, and only slender threads of amber light showed the shape of the windows. Once aboard the private car, we began to observe the taboo that had been fixed on last names. We addressed one another as Ben, Paul, Nelson, Abe." The train started rolling south. One of the bankers had arranged for the group to stay at a fancy hunting club off the coast of Georgia that was deserted in November. Its name was a conspiracy theorist's dream come true: Jekyll Island. Over the next week or so, the group would create a plan to transform the nature of money in America.

Because they thought America needed a central bank, and they knew Americans were wary of both centralization and banking, the cabal cooked up a classic American compromise: a network of not-quite-central banks scattered around the country. Also, they weren't going to be called central banks. They were going to be called "reserve associations." They would be linked together as the Reserve Association of the United States. The reserve associations, like central banks in Europe, would be controlled by private bankers, not by government officials. And they would be able to print dollar bills, and to lend to local banks. The cabal disbursed, and Aldrich released the plan without explaining that it was cooked up in secret by a bunch of bankers.

The plan still seemed like it was cooked up by a bunch of bankers. Congress argued about it. Aldrich retired. The Democrats—the party of Jackson, slayer of the Bank of the United States—won power in Congress. "The ghost of Andrew Jackson stalked before my face in the daytime and haunted my couch for nights," wrote the Democratic congressman who pushed the bill through the House.

The Democrats couldn't live with a bunch of central banks controlled by private bankers. So, contrary to the cabal's plan, the regional reserve associations—now renamed Federal Reserve Banks—would be overseen by a board of governors in Washington, whose members were appointed by the president.

America was on the gold standard, and Congress constrained the Reserve Banks' ability to print paper money. The banks could only create $10 in paper for every $4 worth of gold they had in the vault. And, finally, profoundly, Federal Reserve notes would be "obligations of the United States"—not private money issued by private banks, but government money issued by a new, weird hybrid public-private central bank that was actually twelve different banks but was also, sort of, a central bank.

It was a horse designed by a committee of committees, a camel of a central bank, and if it sounds kind of like a good idea and kind of like a mess, it was. For the next twenty years, the Fed provided the country with a useful currency and smoothed out the seasonal money crunches.

Then, in the crisis that followed the stock market crash of 1929, the fragmented Fed helped to turn what might have been an ordinary economic downturn into the worst economic catastrophe of the twentieth century.

CHAPTER 12

Money Is Dead. Long Live Money

At the core of the gold standard was a simple rule: anyone who wanted to could walk into a Federal Reserve Bank and trade paper dollars for gold—one ounce for every $20.67. By 1933, this rule had become a problem for the Fed.

The country was in the middle of the worst banking panic in its history. People were not only running to their banks to turn their bank deposits into paper dollars; they were running to the Fed to turn their paper dollars into gold. In early March, the panic came to New York—then as now, the center of banking in America. And the New York Fed was about to run out of gold.

So at around one in the morning on March 4, 1933, the head of the New York Fed showed up at the Park Avenue apartment of the governor of New York. He wanted the governor to declare a bank holiday—a weird euphemism that sounds like a cheap package vacation but actually means closing every bank in the state so people can't pull their money out. The governor reluctantly agreed. At 2:30 a.m., he signed an order closing every bank in the state for three days.

This was happening all over the country that morning. The

governor of Illinois closed all the banks in his state. Around dawn, the governor of Pennsylvania did it (and said as he signed the order that he only had 95 cents in his pocket). Massachusetts and New Jersey closed their banks later that morning. Dozens of states had closed their banks in the previous weeks. There were no ATMs, no credit cards. So with banks closed, there was no way for most people in America to get money. That afternoon, in the middle of the worst moment in the history of money in America, with people talking about revolution and the end of capitalism, and soldiers manning machine guns in the streets of Washington, DC, Franklin Delano Roosevelt was sworn in as president of the United States.

Within months, Roosevelt would ignore the advice of his closest advisors and some of the most prominent economists in the country, destroying the very idea of money as it had existed until then, and creating the money we still use today.

How a Shortage of Money Itself Caused the Great Depression

Today, bank deposits in the United States and most other countries are insured by the government. That wasn't always the case; when a bank went out of business, depositors didn't always get their money back. So when people got even a little bit nervous about their bank, they would rush to take their money out. This was an entirely rational thing to do. But once people start rushing to take their money out, no bank can survive. Depositors' money in the bank is never actually in the bank; it's loaned out to borrowers. When a sociologist coined the term "self-fulfilling prophecy" in the 1940s, his first example was a run on a healthy bank.

One thing sure to make depositors nervous is seeing the bank in the next town over go bust. So even in good times the US banking system was like a giant circle of dominoes, with everybody looking anxiously around the circle to see if anything was wobbling. In the 1800s and early 1900s, there were massive, nationwide banking panics every ten to twenty years.

The Federal Reserve had been created in part to prevent these; it had the authority to lend to banks that were fundamentally sound but in danger of suffering a run. Loans from the Fed would allow banks to pay out all the money depositors wanted and prevent a few isolated failures from becoming a nationwide panic.

When the stock market crashed in 1929, the New York Fed did exactly what it was supposed to do: it flooded New York City banks with cheap loans. And it worked! The loans prevented a wave of bank failures, which would have made things even worse.

Still, in 1930, unemployment continued to rise, and spending and prices continued to fall. The head of the New York Fed proposed making it easier for banks to borrow, to try to get the economy going again.

While the mechanics are different today, the Fed still operates on the same basic principle: when the economy starts to get worse, the Fed creates money and makes it cheaper to borrow. This makes it easier for debtors to stay afloat and encourages businesses to borrow money to invest and hire people.

But in 1930, most of the officials at the Federal Reserve Banks scattered around the country didn't want to intervene. The Chicago Fed worried that putting more money into the system would encourage speculative gambling by traders rather than productive investments by businesses. The head of the Dallas Fed warned against "interference with economic trends through artificial methods."

So the Fed sat idle, as falling prices and rising unemployment made it harder for people and businesses to pay their debts. This caused more bank failures. Through the spooky magic of fractional reserve banking, banks had made lots of loans in the 1920s and had turned a relatively small amount of gold and paper bills into a large amount of money in the form of bank deposits. In 1930, that magic ran in reverse. As people pulled their money out of banks, and banks closed, the amount of money in circulation started to fall.

At the same time, people were spending less because they were terrified about the future and wanted to save everything they could. (Also, if you think prices are going to fall, it makes sense to wait to buy stuff, because stuff will be cheaper in the future.) The combination of less money in circulation and less spending caused prices to fall. Falling prices made things even worse for debtors, which meant even more people were unable to pay back their loans, which caused even more banks to fail, which meant that there was even less money in circulation. And so on.

This is called a deflationary spiral. It is not nature taking its course. It is not the necessary correction for a previous bout of speculation. It is a profound, entirely preventable economic disaster caused by money itself. It was what the Fed was supposed to prevent. Instead, the Fed was about to make things worse.

Golden Handcuffs

The international gold standard tied the world's economies together. This was good when they rose together, but in the early '30s, the gold standard was a weight pulling most of Europe and North America to the bottom of the ocean. Banks collapsed across both continents. The center of the financial universe was London, and as people panicked they traded their British pounds for gold. By the fall of 1931 the Bank of England—the same bank that was started just after John Law was tried for murder, and which had by now become the most important central bank in the world—was about to run out of gold. So the Bank of England did something that was both unthinkable and the only thing it could do: it stopped giving people gold in exchange for paper money.

People who had money in the United States looked at this and thought: *Damn! Britain invented the gold standard, and* they *went off it. The United States is going to follow soon.* So they started trading their dollars in for gold, too. In the five weeks after Britain went off the gold standard, people traded in $750 million dollars for gold from the Federal Reserve.

The Federal Reserve knew how to fight this gold drain: it raised interest rates. The higher interest rates are, the higher the incentive for people to keep their money in interest-bearing bank accounts, rather than turning their bank deposits into gold. The higher interest rates worked. People stopped exchanging their dollars for gold.

But raising interest rates also had an unintended (but entirely predictable) consequence: farmers and businesses now had to pay higher interest on their debts, which drove more of them out of business. This in turn made unemployment even worse and made prices fall even more.

Raising interest rates was the exact opposite of what the Fed should have done. Today, the Fed raises interest rates when it is worried that the economy is overheating—when almost everyone has a job, and prices are rising faster and faster. It lowers rates when the economy is weak. By raising interest rates in the fall of 1931, the Fed put its boot on the throat of a country that was lying on the ground after getting the snot kicked out of it for two years. The Chairman of the Fed said the rise in rates was called for "by every known rule," which is to say the Fed did exactly what the gold standard demanded.

Decades later, the economists Milton Friedman and Anna Schwartz pieced together an extraordinarily detailed history of money in America. They showed that the Fed's policy of making money scarcer and raising interest rates—that is to say, following the rules of the gold standard—turned what would have been a nasty but ordinary downturn into a cataclysm. The Fed, and the gold standard it managed, caused the Great Depression.

Today, the gold standard is a thing some people refer to with nostalgia. Politicians sometimes still talk about returning to it. But people who know what they're talking about know this would be a disaster. In 2012, a survey asked dozens of US economists from across the political spectrum about the gold standard. Thirty-nine economists opposed returning to the gold standard. Not a single one supported it. Among today's economists, the gold standard is not a controversial issue. Almost all of them think it's a terrible idea.

But as the Depression unfolded, the link between the gold standard and the spreading catastrophe was still unclear. People thought they were suffering through the inevitable consequences of the boom of the 1920s and the crash of 1929. They thought it had nothing to do with a failure of money itself. In the presidential election of 1932—after three years of falling prices and rising unemployment, after all of the men in hats waiting in line for bread and women holding skinny children in shantytown cardboard houses— President Hoover was still all-in on the gold standard.

"Being forced off the gold standard in the United States means chaos," he said in a campaign speech. "All human experience has demonstrated that that path once taken cannot be stopped, and that the moral integrity of the Government would be sacrificed because ultimately both currency and bonds must become valueless."

His opponent, Franklin Roosevelt, promised "sound money"—a phrase traditionally associated with the gold standard. But Roosevelt never said exactly what he meant by that phrase. Roosevelt was elected in a landslide, in the middle of the greatest monetary crisis in American history, without ever telling anyone what he thought the country should do about money. As far as we can tell, he didn't really know.

You know who knew? Irving damn Fisher. He'd been jumping up and down shouting the answer for twenty years. The essential problem was that the value of money was unstable, and as a result prices were falling. Falling prices were the root cause of the hoarding, and the defaults, and the bank failures. The solution was to get prices to start rising again. But to do that, Fisher knew, Americans needed to change the way they thought about money itself.

"The End of Western Civilization"

Fisher was no longer entirely alone in his views. The most famous economist in England, John Maynard Keynes, was influenced by Fisher. And in the United States, Fisher had on his side a few businessmen and a relatively unknown agricultural economist named George Warren. In the fall of 1932, this crew created the humbly named Committee for the Nation to Rebuild Prices and Purchasing Power, which was a successor to Fisher's Stable Money Association. "The committee," the historian Arthur Schlesinger Jr. wrote, "lent a sort of pseudo-respectability to the inflation drive."

Pseudo, indeed. Warren was a Cornell economist who studied agriculture and had spent years trying to figure out how to get hens to lay more eggs. When the price of produce and meat started falling in the '20s, Warren became obsessed with the relationship between gold and commodity prices. He spent years gathering and analyzing centuries of data. Eventually, he was persuaded by Fisher's basic argument that the only way out of the Depression was to raise prices, and the only way to raise prices was to break the hundred-year-old promise of the gold standard.

Warren happened to know Roosevelt personally. He had consulted with him about the trees on his estate in upstate New York and advised him on agriculture when Roosevelt was governor. After the election, Warren and Fisher both corresponded with Roosevelt and met with his top aides to push their views on money.

The day after Roosevelt was inaugurated, Warren got on a little private plane (the same model Lindbergh had flown across the Atlantic six years before) and flew to Washington to try to get in to see the president in person.

In the weeks leading up to this moment, things had gone from bad to insane. Now, on top of all the human suffering of the Depression—the unemployment and hunger and homelessness—a wave of bank runs worse than any that had come before broke out across the country. As banks collapsed and states declared bank holidays, money itself began to disappear.

People improvised. More than a hundred cities printed paper IOUs that circulated as temporary money. A Detroit department store bartered with farmers—a dress for three barrels of herring, three pairs of shoes for a five-hundred-pound sow. A boxing promoter at Madison Square Garden bartered tickets for "hats, shoes, cigars, combs, soap, chisels, kettles, sacks of potatoes, and foot balm."

The most famous line Roosevelt delivered the day he was inaugurated was perhaps the perfect response to the biggest bank run in American history: "The only thing we have to fear is fear itself." In the middle of a gargantuan bank run—the canonical self-fulfilling prophecy—fear itself is the essential problem.

Warren got in to see Roosevelt at the White House at 10:30 p.m. the next night. A few hours later, sitting in his study, smoking a cigarette in an ivory holder, in his second act as president, Roosevelt signed a proclamation that temporarily closed every bank in America. Warren was thrilled.

Reporters suggested Roosevelt had just taken America off the gold standard. Will Woodin, Roosevelt's Treasury Secretary, wasn't having it. "It is ridiculous and misleading to say we have gone off the gold standard," Woodin said. "We are definitely on the gold standard. Gold merely cannot be obtained for several days." Woodin's point for the reporters was that America was really, really on the gold standard, could not be more on the gold standard if it tried, and that America basically was even more on the gold standard than ever.

In March 1933, Fisher and Warren were still outsiders. The nation's top economists and bankers, along with Roosevelt's own advisors, were still nearly unanimous in their belief that the United States needed to stay on the gold standard. Woodin wanted to make that clear. But Roosevelt wasn't sure. Three days after he closed every bank in America and locked down the country's gold supply, he held his first press conference, telling reporters off the record, "As long as nobody asks me whether we are off the gold standard or gold basis, that's all right."

That week, while the banks were still closed, Congress rushed through an emergency banking law. It spelled out how officials would decide which banks could reopen. It also gave the government the right to force all Americans to sell their gold to the government.

The next weekend, Roosevelt gave his first national radio address. It was a moment of profound, even existential, peril for the country. People were seriously discussing the collapse of capitalism, and American farmers were in open revolt over falling prices. But Roosevelt didn't talk about any of that. Instead, the new president went on the radio and said: "I want to talk for a few minutes with the people of the United States about banking." And then—in the middle of everything—he gave the country a really basic primer on how banks and money work.

"First of all, let me state the simple fact that when you deposit money in a bank, the bank does not put the money into a safe-deposit vault…the bank puts your money to work to keep the wheels of industry and of agriculture turning around…the total amount of all the currency in the country is only a small fraction of the total deposits in all of the banks…

"What, then, happened during the last few days of February and the first few days of March? Because of undermined confidence on the part of the public, there was a general rush by a large portion of our population to turn bank deposits into currency or gold—a rush so great that the soundest banks could not get enough currency to meet the demand."

Federal officials, Roosevelt said, were now examining every bank in the country. Banks that were sound—the vast majority of the banks—would reopen. More than anything, Roosevelt wanted to break the cycle of fear that had led to one bank run after another. "After all," he said, "there is an element in the readjustment of our financial system more important than currency, more important than gold, and that is the confidence of the people.... Let us unite in banishing fear.... Together we cannot fail."

Roosevelt understood that money is money because we believe it's money. When people lost confidence in their banks, they ceased to think of their deposits as money, so they withdrew their deposits in the form of paper bills. When they lost confidence in paper, they turned it into gold. These changes weren't neutral. With each step—from deposits to paper, from paper to gold—America was sliding backward into a world with less money that worked less well. It was this slide that Roosevelt was trying to reverse.

The next day, banks started to reopen. Once again, people lined up outside their banks. But this time, they weren't there to take money out. They were there to put money in. It was a bank run in reverse! The banking holiday and the fireside chat had worked. Once people trusted banks, people turned their paper back into bank deposits because they once again believed bank deposits were money.

The bank holiday ended gradually, as one bank after another opened back up. But many people were still scared, prices were still depressed, and lending was still weak. A few weeks later, Roosevelt dropped another bomb. He issued executive order 6102:

All persons are hereby required to deliver on or before May 1, 1933... to any member bank of the Federal Reserve System all gold coin, gold bullion and gold certificates now owned by them... Whoever willfully violates any provision of this Executive Order or of these regulations or of any rule, regulation or license issued thereunder may be fined not more than $10,000, or... imprisoned for not more than ten years, or both...

Roosevelt, like John Law before him, made it a crime for people simply to own gold. You could go to jail, the president said, just for keeping a few hundred dollars of gold coins in your desk drawer. (People could still own jewelry, and a token amount of coins.) Just imagine the response today if a president announced that all Americans had to turn in their gold. Yet in a sign of just how insane the spring of 1933 was, this wasn't even the biggest moment of the month. That came a few weeks later.

At the time, a farm bill was working its way through Congress. An Oklahoma senator was pushing a radical amendment that would give the president the power to change, for the first time in a hundred years, the value of the dollar in terms of gold. This was, of course, anathema. A dollar was defined as a fixed amount of gold. This was the essential, unchangeable truth of the gold standard, the bedrock on which the whole system was built.

But on April 18, Roosevelt gathered his closest economic advisors and, to their shock, he said he was going to back the amendment. With his support, it would almost certainly become law. "Congratulate me," Roosevelt said. "We are off the gold standard."

Then, as one advisor put it, "all hell broke loose in the room." One banker-turned-advisor told Roosevelt that he was leading the country into "uncontrolled inflation and complete chaos." Roosevelt's own budget director agreed. The two men "fought like tigers—paced up and down and argued every which way," trying to persuade Roosevelt to change his mind. The president laughed it off. He pulled a ten-dollar bill out of his pocket. "How do I know that's any good?" he said. "The fact that I think it is, makes it good." They argued until midnight. The president, unfazed, went to bed. "Well," the budget director said, as the advisors walked out of the White House, "this is the end of Western civilization."

"I am now one of the happiest men in the world," Fisher wrote to his wife the next day when he heard the news. "Happy that we are to get back prosperity, happy to have had a share in the work which turned the scales and in the laying of the foundations years ago. I feel that this week marks the culmination of my life work. Even if I had no more of life, I would feel that what I have had has been as worthwhile as any man has a right to expect."

Roosevelt's approach to money was ad hoc, ill informed, and contrary to what most smart, well-meaning, well-informed people thought he should do. Also, it worked. Not beautifully, not perfectly. But it definitely worked.

The spring of 1933 was the bottom of the Depression—the worst moment in the worst economic catastrophe in American history. After Roosevelt closed the banks, confiscated everyone's gold, and abandoned the gold standard, everything started to turn around. Prices started rising. This finally eased the burden on debtors. Unemployment started falling. Incomes and the stock market started rising. The rise was slow, and uneven, and there were lots more problems, and the United States wouldn't fully recover until World War II. Yet the trend was clear.

Decades later, when economic historians looked back, not just at the United States, but also at Britain and France and Germany and Japan, they saw an unmistakable correlation. In country after country, the economy started to improve after the government gave up on the gold standard. And, economists have concluded, there was a cause-and-effect relationship. The gold standard locked countries in a terrible economic cycle. Breaking the link to gold broke the cycle.

The world did remain on a pseudo gold standard for decades; foreign governments could still trade dollars for gold (at a rate of $35 per ounce, as set by Roosevelt in 1934), but ordinary people could no longer do so. Finally, in 1971, the United States broke the link to gold entirely. It became the job of the Federal Reserve to manage the value of the dollar—not in terms of gold, but in terms of the stuff ordinary Americans buy. In other words, America (and every other country) finally started thinking of money the way Irving Fisher wanted us to.

But the essential moment was 1933. In the fall of that year, Roosevelt wrote to a Harvard economist, a close advisor who was insisting that Roosevelt immediately go back on the gold standard: "You place a former artificial gold standard among nations above human suffering and the crying needs of your own country." The essential word in that sentence is not "suffering" or "crying." It's "artificial."

The believers in the gold standard gave it the power of nature. They didn't so much argue as simply took as given the fact that gold-as-money was the natural order of things, and that any other policy was not only unwise but also unnatural and therefore doomed to fail.

Roosevelt recognized that there was nothing natural about the gold standard; it was as artificial as any other monetary arrangement. The gold standard was a choice people had made—even if they didn't recognize it as a choice. Roosevelt's great genius was simply to say: we can choose something else.

V

TWENTY-FIRST-CENTURY MONEY

The history of money is the history of banks and governments and ordinary people fighting over who gets to do what. As it turns out, this is also the present of money—the story of shadow banking and the euro and, inevitably, bitcoin.

CHAPTER 13

How Two Guys in a Room Invented a New Kind of Money

Here is the standard story of the 2008 financial crisis:

1. Shady lenders gave ridiculous mortgages to unqualified buyers of overpriced houses.

2. The ridiculous mortgages were then bundled together, sliced up, and sold off to investors.

3. When housing prices started to fall, the unqualified buyers couldn't pay back the ridiculous mortgages.

4. The investors who bought the bundles of ridiculous mortgages blew up and took the economy down with them.

This story has the virtues of being true and dramatic. But it is incomplete. It is only part of the story of the crisis. The ridiculous mortgages alone would not have been enough to blow up the entire economy. There is a whole other part of the story that's almost never told.

The other part is a story about money itself—a new kind of money that started flowing through a new kind of banking system that nobody quite knew was a banking system. This new kind of money drove the bananas rise of finance in the late twentieth and early twenty-first centuries. Also, this new kind of money helped a relatively small corner of the US mortgage market blow up the global economy. And there is a fundamental problem with this new kind of money that nobody has entirely fixed, and unless it gets fixed, it could blow up the world again.

This chapter is that part of the story.

The Two Guys

"I always had an attraction to money," Bruce Bent said. He started collecting empty soda bottles and turning them in for the deposit money when he was an eight-year-old kid in postwar Long Island. He tried being a paperboy, but the math just never made sense. "Delivering papers was a crap job: too much work, not enough pay." So he got a job at the grocery store. "I was making $70 a week when I was 14. Outstanding money."

After high school he became a mailman, like his dad. He spent six months in the Marines as a reserve, went on to graduate from St. John's University, and, like lots of people who are attracted to money, found his way to a job in finance. "I went down to Wall Street and was the flunky to the managing partners."

A few years later, he got a job in the investment department at an insurance company. He started on the same day as the man who would be his boss, Harry Brown. Brown was a Harvard graduate and the grandson of a federal judge and just a very different kind of guy than Bent.

They met for the first time on their first day, in the office of Harry's boss (Bent's boss's boss). A few minutes later—which is to say, a few minutes after they'd met—Harry looked at Bruce and said to the big boss: "I don't like him. I don't want him working in my department."

"Why not?"

"He's a New York City wiseass and I don't want him in my department."

"Deal with him."

In the end, Bent and Brown loved working with each other. A few years later, they left their jobs to start their own company: Brown and Bent. They thought they would match insurance companies that had money to invest with companies that needed to borrow. But business was slow.

Bent had a wife and two kids and two mortgages. He bought a thrift-store bike to save on bus fare. He rode his bike to the train and rode the train to work and sat across from Brown in the office, where they kicked ideas back and forth. "We were trying to find something that was a money-earning experience," Bent said.

After a few years of this marginal existence, Bent and Brown saw an opportunity. Federal regulations put in place in 1933 capped interest rates on bank savings accounts and prohibited banks from paying any interest at all on checking accounts. But people who had lots of money and were willing to tie it up for a few weeks or months could get more interest from opening savings accounts of at least $100,000 or buying short-term government debt known as Treasury bills (or T-bills).

Bent and Brown decided to figure out how investors who didn't want to tie up their money, or who couldn't make such a big investment, could get the higher interest rates offered by T-bills and jumbo savings accounts. One afternoon, Bent had an idea. "I looked up at Brown and said, 'Why not a mutual fund?'" Bent said. "He said he didn't know anything about mutual funds. I said, 'I don't know anything about mutual funds either, but I think it would work.'"

Mutual funds are pools of money that typically are invested in stocks or bonds. If you have a retirement account, there's a very good chance that you are an investor in one or more mutual funds. When investors buy shares in a mutual fund, they are actually buying an ownership stake in all the stocks or bonds (or both) that the fund owns. The value of the mutual fund shares rises and falls every day with the value of the stocks and bonds in the fund.

Brown and Bent wanted to create a mutual fund that would feel like money in the bank—not like an investment in stocks or bonds. They wanted it to have all the convenience of a checking account, but with a higher interest rate for savers. So they made a few tweaks to the mutual fund model.

Investors would buy shares in their fund. The fund would then take investors' money and lend it out—to the government, in the form of Treasury bills, and to banks, in the form of big savings accounts. These were short-term, ultra-safe investments. So safe, in fact, that the price of the mutual fund shares didn't need to fluctuate every day like funds that owned stocks or riskier bonds. Brown and Bent decided to set the share price at $1 per share. And they were able to use an accounting system such that, outside of some catastrophe, they would be able to leave the price at $1 per share. Just like money in the bank.

They wanted to call their fund the "Savings Fund," but the Securities and Exchange Commission (SEC), which regulates mutual funds, wouldn't let them. So they called it the "Reserve Fund," similarly boring, which is what they were going for.

The Fund opened for business in 1972. By the end of 1973, they were managing $100 million. Within a few years, a bunch of competing funds had sprung up. This new kind of fund came to be called a money-market fund. Pretty soon, you could write checks against your money-market fund—which is to say, you could use your money-market money to buy stuff. Just like money in the bank!

The Big Banks Get In on It

Corporations with extra cash on hand started parking hundreds of millions of dollars in money-market funds. By 1982, ten years after Bent and Brown came up with the idea in their tiny office, money funds had more than $200 billion, with billions more flowing in every year.

The funds suddenly had more cash than they knew what to do with. Bent and Brown stuck with investing in large bank deposits and government debt, but other fund managers started looking for new options. Some funds started buying something called "commercial paper," which was basically a way to make short-term loans to safe, stable companies. In the 1980s, money-market funds became the biggest buyers of commercial paper.

Vast flows of money were now shifting from banks to money funds. So Citibank, one of the biggest banks in the country, figured out how to do the thing banks do: get in the middle of a vast flow of money. With a bunch of complicated legal and financial maneuvering, Citi invented something called "asset-backed commercial paper." It was a new way for money-market funds to lend money to companies that weren't safe enough to issue commercial paper.

Soon other banks jumped in. By the early '90s, billions of dollars were flowing into asset-backed commercial paper, and banks were selling more every month.

Bent, who'd started it all, thought commercial paper was too risky for money-market funds. "Commercial paper is anathema to the concept of the money fund," he told a reporter in 2001. "People prostituted the concept by putting garbage in the funds and reaching for yield."

Bent's Reserve Fund still invested only in government-backed debt and certificates of deposit from old-fashioned banks. "We consider it prudent rather than plain," Bent's son, who was president of the family business by this point, told the *Wall Street Journal*.

In a few years, the Bents would quietly abandon this worldview at exactly the wrong time.

The Money Boom

The last decades of the twentieth century were an extraordinary financial boom, and lots of rich people and corporations and pension funds and foreign governments found themselves with the pleasant problem of having more cash than they knew what to do with.

This wasn't money they wanted to invest. This was money that they essentially wanted to put in their checking account. Money they would need to make payroll next week, or cover the retirement checks sent out next month, or whatever. Since government insurance on checking accounts topped out at $100,000, there wasn't an obvious place to put this cash. The classic thing to do in this setting is to buy very short-term Treasury debt, but there was so much cash to park that there just weren't enough Treasuries to go around.

A lot of these people invested in money-market funds; some imitated the funds and invested on their own. The money-market funds, with more money than they knew what to do with, turned around and started lending huge amounts of money to investment banks on Wall Street. (Investment banks, despite their name, aren't like regular banks; they're not really in the business of taking deposits and making loans, and they don't have the government guarantees that regular banks have.) All this money innocently looking for a safe, short-term home was the air that inflated the great finance bubble of the early twenty-first century.

The aughts come. The housing boom is booming. Wildly unqualified borrowers are taking out absurdly large mortgages on overpriced houses. But in this version of the story we are starting a step earlier. We are looking at where the money that is being loaned to the unqualified buyers of the overpriced houses is coming from. The answer, as you have already guessed: money-market mutual funds! Pension funds and corporations that needed to park their cash! This new kind of money flowing in vast sums through money-market mutual funds and asset-backed commercial paper and investment banks was the money that inflated the bubble.

In late 2006, home prices stopped rising and corporate treasurers and money-market funds started getting nervous. So they started asking for their money back from some of the investment funds that had borrowed money (via asset-backed commercial paper) to invest in mortgages. In a few cases, the investors couldn't come up with the money. When that happened, lots more people started asking for their money back.

To the outside world, this looked like some super-wonky thing going on in some arcane corner of the financial world. But to Paul McCulley, it looked like something else—something much more worrying.

Shadow Banking

McCulley was an economist who worked at a giant investment firm called PIMCO. He looked out across this world of money-market funds and asset-backed commercial paper and said: this is not just a bunch of arcane investment vehicles. It's an entire banking system that nobody quite recognizes as a banking system.

A bank borrows money from depositors, who can ask for their money back at any time. Then the bank turns around and makes long-term loans. The fundamental bank thing that the bank is doing is borrowing short-term and lending long-term. The money-market funds and asset-backed commercial paper markets were doing the same thing: taking money that investors could demand at a moment's notice and turning around and lending it out. In the shadows of the regulated banking system, a whole new system of quasi-banks had sprung up. And now there was a problem.

"What's going on is really simple," McCulley told a room full of central bankers at a meeting in the summer of 2007. "We're having a run on the shadow banking system." It was the first time anyone had used that term to describe this new universe: shadow banking.

Everybody thought we had solved bank runs in the Depression.

The government started guaranteeing the money people deposited in the bank so people didn't need to rush to the bank at the first sign of trouble anymore. The Fed stood ready to lend to sound banks that were in a temporary crunch. The government stood behind everybody's bank account. Our money was safe.

But without anybody really realizing it, a parallel banking structure had sprung up. It was massive, and it was global. It allowed hedge funds and investment banks to borrow more and more and more money, to make bigger and bigger bets. It provided a lot of the money to people buying homes in the United States. It had all of the risk of traditional banking—the potential for a run that could wreck the entire economy—with none of the safety net.

"The short-term IOUs that are issued by shadow banks...are called cash equivalents," Morgan Ricks, a trader turned law professor, wrote later. "Corporate treasurers and other businesspeople just call them cash." In other words, shadow banks were creating real money.

By 2007, shadow banking was bigger than traditional banking. And the depositors in the shadow banks—the corporate treasurers and money-market funds and pension funds that had trillions of dollars of cash—were starting to demand their money back. It was the start of the biggest bank run in history.

The run hit Bear Stearns first. Bear was a small, risk-loving investment bank that borrowed tons of money from money-market funds and used it to buy mortgage-backed bonds. In March 2008, the funds decided the risk of lending to Bear was no longer worth it. Fidelity, the biggest money-market fund manager in America, had been lending Bear nearly $10 billion. In a single week, they demanded every penny of it back.

This is the moment in the bank run when all the depositors line up outside the bank to withdraw their money. It's the moment when the British navy official says these notes are not money. But instead of 5,000 people with deposits of a few thousand dollars each, it was 50 institutions with deposits of hundreds of millions each. Bear had taken the borrowed money and used it to buy billions of dollars in mortgage-backed bonds. Now nobody wanted to buy those bonds. Bear Stearns' depositors—including the money-market funds—wanted their money back, and Bear Stearns didn't have it.

Bear Stearns wasn't a commercial bank. It didn't hold deposits for regular people and wasn't supposed to be able to borrow from the Fed. But the Fed invoked a legal provision that said it could lend to anyone in "unusual and exigent circumstances," and loaned $13 billion to Bear. The Fed was following Walter Bagehot's nineteenth-century advice to "lend to merchants, to minor bankers, to 'this man and that man.'" The central bank was pouring money into the shadow bank run, acting as lender of last resort.

The loan allowed Bear to open for business on Friday. That weekend, in a shotgun wedding, JPMorgan Chase bought Bear Stearns outright. As part of the deal, the Fed agreed to buy $30 billion in mortgage bonds from Bear Stearns. And then Bear Stearns ceased to exist. The bonds, in the end, were fine. The Fed eventually got its money back, with interest.

A few months later, the bank run came for another investment bank: Lehman Brothers. Lehman was Bear Stearns but bigger. The company owned an enormous quantity of crappy mortgage-backed securities. It had borrowed so, so much money. In September 2008, approximately everybody who had been parking their money with Lehman decided they wanted it back. Lehman didn't have the money. It had a bunch of mortgage-backed bonds that nobody wanted to buy. Early in the morning on Monday, September 15, Lehman declared bankruptcy.

Bruce Bent Breaks the Buck

Three days before Lehman filed for bankruptcy, the *Wall Street Journal* ran a small story, deep inside the paper, about an obscure regulatory question in the money-market fund industry. The story quoted Bruce Bent, inventor of the money-market fund, arguing once again that other money fund managers were taking too many risks. "Lest we forget, the purpose of the money fund is to bore the investor into a sound night's sleep," he said.

Bent loved this theme, and he was hitting it hard. In the Reserve Funds' annual report a few months earlier, he had written:

> One year has passed since the ... [subprime] crisis shook the foundation of our markets, which has investors questioning the safety of their money funds. Good! We are pleased to report that you, and the markets in general, have embraced the very concept and foundation on which The Reserve was founded, an unwavering discipline focused on protecting your principal ...

But readers who looked past Bent's letter and into the details of the report would have noticed something surprising. The Reserve Primary Fund was no longer the "prudent rather than plain" fund that limited itself to investing in boring bank deposits and government-backed bonds. Now the firm was taking investors' money and buying tens of billions of dollars of commercial paper—just the sort of riskier investment Bent had once said money-market funds should avoid.

On the morning of September 15, 2008, the Bents' Reserve Fund (now technically called the Reserve Primary Fund) owned $785 million in commercial paper issued by Lehman Brothers. Which is to say that Lehman Brothers, which had just declared bankruptcy, owed the Reserve Fund $785 million. It represented a little more than 1 percent of the total amount of money in the fund. That is just a tiny sliver! Even if the Primary Fund could recover no money at all from Lehman—and they could almost certainly recover something—the other 99 percent of the fund would be fine. If the Reserve Fund were a normal mutual fund, this would have been a nonevent. Mutual funds lose or gain 1 percent all the time.

But the Reserve Fund was not a normal mutual fund. It was a money-market fund. Despite the standard warnings that the fund might lose money, people did not think of their money in the fund as an investment. They thought of their money in the fund as their money. You put in a dollar, you get back a dollar whenever you want it. If the fund were to lose 1 percent of its value, investors wouldn't get all their money back. This, for a money-market fund, is a disaster known as "breaking the buck."

The savvy institutional investors who knew what was going on rushed to pull their money out of the Reserve Fund. By midmorning, just hours after Lehman declared bankruptcy, investors had redeemed $10 billion—ten times as much as in a typical morning. Like a bank, the Fund didn't have that cash on hand. It had a bunch of bonds and commercial paper it had to sell to get the money. So, at 10:10 a.m., the bank that managed redemptions for the Reserve Fund stopped giving investors their money back.

Over the next few hours, depositors tried to withdraw another $8 billion. But the Reserve Fund couldn't sell assets fast enough to come up with the money. The shadow bank run was hidden from the public, but it's audible in the internal phone calls fund executives were having that day. (The calls were later made public in court records.)

"We're in the hole for about eight," one executive says. (Terrifyingly, he's speaking in billions of dollars.)

And then a minute later:

"How much have we raised?"

"We've raised about a billion. That's all we've been able to raise..."

"Oh, my gosh."

"Yeah."

"Well, that's really bad."

This is the morning Lehman went bankrupt. The biggest financial crisis in seventy years. Everybody is demanding their money back everywhere. All of the shadow banks are suddenly trying to sell all of their assets. But nobody's buying!

As these two guys are talking on the phone, they actually see the run happening in front of them. Giant companies that have parked their cash with the Reserve Fund are calling and asking for their money back. One of those companies was ADP, which does HR-type stuff for other companies.

"Oh, fuck....frickin' ADP just took out fucking 213," one of guys on the call says. He means $213 million.

"It's not going to—nothing's going to go," the other guy says.

This is the part of the bank run where the teller puts down the glass in the window and walks away while depositors frantically scream for their money.

"Those customers are not going to get their money tonight."

"That's going to be the kiss of death."

All that day and into Tuesday morning, the Bents tried to borrow money. They tried to sell a chunk of their firm. But it didn't happen. They couldn't come up with the money. Tuesday afternoon, the fund announced: "The value of the debt securities issued by Lehman Brothers Holdings, Inc....and held by the Primary Fund has been valued at zero effective 4:00PM New York time today. As a result, the NAV [net asset value] of the Primary Fund, effective as of 4:00PM, is $0.97 per share." The Reserve Primary Fund had broken the buck.

As the news spread, investors started pulling hundreds of billions of dollars from other money-market funds. To meet the redemptions, the funds had to sell their assets—including their commercial paper. But nobody wanted to buy commercial paper. Nobody wanted to lend, even to sound borrowers.

"Suddenly GE and Caterpillar and Boeing were having trouble borrowing money to make payroll and pay suppliers....Everybody is running from all forms of commercial paper," a lawyer who worked at the New York Fed told me. "One of our senior economists said, 'Well, that's not rational behavior.' I ran into the bathroom and dry heaved."

Shadow Money Is Real Money

On Friday, three days after the Reserve Fund broke the buck, President George W. Bush gave a speech at the White House Rose Garden. "The Department of the Treasury is acting to restore confidence in a key element of America's financial system: money-market mutual funds," the president said. Then he said the government was going to offer insurance for money-market funds.

In the 1930s, the government had put a fence around ordinary people's bank accounts and said: Okay, what's inside this fence is no longer a loan to the bank that you, the depositor, may or may not get back. Your bank deposit is your money. The government is going to insure the money inside this fence to make sure you get your money back. And we're going to regulate the hell out of banks, and make them pay for the insurance, to keep that money safe.

Now, President Bush was essentially admitting that money—the thing the government had promised to keep safe—had jumped the fence. The dollars people had invested in money-market funds were no longer investments that people might or might not get back. They were now money, guaranteed by the United States, just like money in the bank or a gold coin in a locked box guarded by a soldier with a gun. "For every dollar invested in an insured fund, you will be able to take a dollar out," the president said.

The president's next sentence was boring but extraordinarily important: "The Federal Reserve is also taking steps to provide additional liquidity to money-market mutual funds, which will help ease pressure on our financial markets." This was the other half of the money bargain, previously only available to banks: the Fed as lender of last resort. Now, the president was saying, the Fed stood ready to lend against the commercial paper that the money-market funds held and that nobody, but nobody, wanted to buy.

Two days later, Morgan Stanley and Goldman Sachs—the last two freestanding big investment banks—became bank holding companies. That meant they now got all of the delicious Federal Reserve lending of last resort that classic banks could get. Citibank and Bank of America, which had gotten into shadow banking by directing hundreds of billions of dollars into asset-backed commercial paper, would get bailouts in the form of hundreds of billions of dollars in government loans and guarantees in the months that followed.

Shadow banking, and the shadow money it created, managed to get all of the safety net, after going decades without paying any of the cost. Shadow money was now real money.

Money-market funds survived, but the Reserve Fund did not. It was wound down, and investors received 99 cents on the dollar.

Money and the Next Crisis

In 2009, the Group of Thirty—an absurdly elite organization whose thirty members include Nobel Prize–winning economists, people who have run every major central bank in the world, and the heads of several of the planet's biggest banks—suggested a future for money-market funds. If it walks like a duck, swims like a duck, and quacks like a duck, they said, we should regulate it like a duck.

"Money market mutual funds wishing to continue to offer bank-like services..." a report from the group said, "should be required to reorganize as special-purpose banks, with appropriate prudential regulation..." If, on the other hand, money funds didn't want to be regulated like banks, they could stop letting people write checks on their accounts and stop showing a constant value of $1 per share—in short, they could stop acting like banks that held people's money for safekeeping.

The companies that ran money-market mutual funds wanted to

keep acting like banks without being regulated like banks. "Fundamentally changing the nature of money market funds (and in the process eviscerating a product that has been so successful for both investors and the U.S. money market) goes too far and will create new risks," an industry group wrote a few months later. (The use of "so successful" was an impressive show of chutzpah in 2009, less than a year after the run on money funds.)

The government insurance issued during the crisis was allowed to expire once the crisis passed. People argued for years over what to do about money funds. In the end, some new rules were put in place, but the industry got much of what it wanted.

Funds that are open only to big investors like companies and endowments do have to report daily swings in value, down to a fraction of a penny. But funds for ordinary investors still use the same accounting methods to show a constant dollar value for investors. People can still write checks on their accounts. Money-market funds are not regulated like banks, but for most people money in a money fund still feels like money in the bank.

In the spring of 2020, as the coronavirus pandemic spread around the world, people once again started frantically pulling billions of dollars out of money-market funds. And the US government once again rushed to protect the funds. "It's just frustrating that we never really fixed this stuff to begin with," Sheila Bair, a former regulator, said. "The industry lobbyists came in and persuaded regulators to do half measures. And we're back in the soup again."

✳ ✳ ✳

One essential lesson of the Panic of 2008 is this: follow the money. Not in the traditional sense of looking for the place where the money is going, but in the shadow money sense of looking for the place where new kinds of quasi-money are being created. Look for the place where people are making loans that don't feel like loans— they feel like money in the bank, which can be withdrawn at full face value at a moment's notice.

What is the thing that is like a piece of paper from a goldsmith in 1690, or a deposit in a bank in 1930, or a money-market fund balance in 2007? When everybody who holds that thing decides to cash it in at once, the world will get very ugly very fast.

CHAPTER 14

A Brief History of the Euro (and Why the Dollar Works Better)

We remember the fall of the Berlin Wall in a nostalgic haze. It was the beginning of that moment of sweet delusion, between the fall of the Soviet Union and the attacks on the World Trade Center and Pentagon, when the good guys had won and the bad guys had lost and Germany got to be one country again and everything was going to be okay.

But at the time, the Germans' neighbors were terrified. The French, British, and Soviets thought German reunification could bring back the aggressive, expansionist Germany that had destroyed Europe less than fifty years earlier.

"Help me to prevent German unification," Mikhail Gorbachev told François Mitterrand, the president of France, when the wall came down. "Otherwise I will be replaced by a soldier; otherwise, you will bear the responsibility for war." When Mitterrand met with Margaret Thatcher, she pulled out a map showing territories in Eastern Europe that had shifted from Germany to Poland after World War II. "They'll take all of that, and Czechoslovakia, too," she said.

But Mitterrand didn't want to push Germany away; he wanted to grab Germany in a European bear hug. And he wanted to use money to do it. He wanted to create a new kind of money managed not by a single country, but shared by a collective of European nations. It was a radical idea, but Mitterrand thought it was Europe's only hope to avoid being economically dominated by Germany. "Without a common currency," Mitterrand told Thatcher, "we are all of us—you and we—already subordinate to the Germans' will."

The story of how a bunch of countries gave up their own money and decided to share a single currency isn't just about money. It's about what it means to be a nation. At its center, the question boils down to this: What does a country lose when it gives up control over its money?

A Wild Experiment That People Didn't Want to Admit Was a Wild Experiment

Less than a month after the fall of the wall, Mitterrand offered a deal to Helmut Kohl, the German chancellor. If Germany agreed to a common currency, France would support reunification. If Germany didn't agree, France would oppose reunification—and the UK and the Soviet Union would go along with France, leaving Germany surrounded as it was before World War I. "We will return to the world of 1913," Mitterrand told Kohl.

Giving up a currency is a big deal for any country. For Germany, it was almost unimaginable. In the decades since World War II, the Germans had largely given up on nationalism (for good reason!) and focused instead on creating a strong economy and, above all, stable money. They rebuilt their country around their currency, the deutschmark. "The deutschmark is our flag," Kohl told Mitterrand. "It is the essential part of our national pride; we don't have much else."

The Europeans had been talking about sharing a currency for decades, but they hadn't made much progress. Karl Otto Pöhl, the head of the Bundesbank, Germany's central bank, said he thought it would take a hundred years for Europe to get a single currency. When he was appointed to a committee on creating a shared currency, he read the newspaper in the middle of committee meetings to show his disdain. It was a dick move, but he did it for a reason: there were profound, seemingly irreconcilable differences in the way the French and the Germans thought money should work. Deciding suddenly to have the same money would be stranger than deciding suddenly to speak the same language. It would be more like deciding suddenly to have the same culture. How do you even do that?

The French saw money as a tool elected officials should use to achieve their desired ends. France's central bank, the Banque de France, took its orders from French politicians. The politicians often wanted to stimulate the economy by creating more money and driving down interest rates, even if it meant higher inflation.

The Germans, on the other hand, thought money couldn't be trusted to politicians. The temptation for the government to create more and more money, and drive inflation higher and higher, seemed too great. The Germans had lived through hyperinflation in the 1920s, when the value of the mark fell by the minute. People would walk into pubs and order two beers at once, because by the time they finished the first one, the price would have gone up for the second.

The Germans learned how tenuous the value of money is, and

after the war they rebuilt their economy around protecting that value. They were willing to suffer through recessions rather than risk inflation. Politicians appointed technocrats to run the central bank, the Bundesbank, and then left them alone. "Not all Germans believe in God," a French politician said, "but they all believe in the Bundesbank."

So when the technocrat running the Bundesbank got sent to some meeting to talk about giving up the deutschmark to share a currency with a bunch of flaky Europeans who didn't know the value of money, he read the newspaper.

And when the French finance minister gave a speech to a roomful of German bankers in the fall of 1989, with the head of the Bundesbank sitting in the front row, he said: "No to technocracy! Yes to democracy! Central bankers have no right to be given superior authority!"

Three days after that speech, the Berlin Wall fell. President Mitterrand told Chancellor Kohl that Europe would let Germany be one Germany if Germany would let Europe have one currency. Kohl didn't really have a choice; reunifying Germany was hard enough without worrying about a bunch of hostile neighbors. So he took the deal. The month after the fall of the Wall, Kohl went against the wishes of Germany's central bank and many of its people and agreed to give up his country's precious currency.

Pöhl, the head of the Bundesbank, started negotiating terms of surrender for the deutschmark. He wanted the new currency to be controlled by a European central bank that was run by technocrats whose main job was fighting inflation (not stimulating the economy), and who were not answerable to politicians. Ideally, the bank's headquarters would be in Germany, for safekeeping. Basically, he wanted to keep the deutschmark, but let other countries use it. But even that was not enough.

The value of money, Pöhl and his colleagues explained in 1990, would soon depend on the actions of every single country that shared the currency. For the system to work, all the countries needed to keep deficits and inflation low. But in the long run that wouldn't be enough. A common currency would only work, the German central bankers wrote, if the countries agreed to a "comprehensive political union"—if they became more like a single country, a United States of Europe.

The Europeans agreed to meet the first part of Pöhl's demands. The new currency would be controlled by an independent central bank charged with fighting inflation, and headquartered in Germany. Citizens would be able to cross borders freely in order to work. But there wouldn't be a single, overarching European government that collected taxes and redistributed money across the eurozone. The Europeans weren't really ready to create a United States of Europe.

So hundreds of millions of people were subjected to a wild experiment that no one in power admitted was a wild experiment: What happens when twelve countries, with vastly different economies, share a single kind of money?

The Euro Is a Miracle!

Just before midnight, on December 31, 2001, 10,000 people gathered around a statue of the euro symbol in Frankfurt, outside the headquarters of the new European Central Bank. At midnight, euro bills and coins became legal tender. There were fireworks and speeches. The rollout, which involved printing billions of euro notes and changing over tens of thousands of ATMs, was a logistical triumph. By the end of February people had stopped using lira and francs and marks and pesetas and drachmas. For the first time since the fall of the Roman Empire, all of Western Europe was using the same kind of money.

The dream was coming true. Not just in the symbolic sense, of the pieces of paper with generic bridges on them, but in the economic sense as well. For a long time, people and governments in countries at the core of Western Europe (Germany, France, the Netherlands) had been able to borrow money more cheaply than those on the periphery (Portugal, Spain, Italy, Greece). The countries on the periphery had a history of higher inflation and higher deficits, and lenders demanded higher interest rates to compensate for that risk. Because low deficits and low inflation were conditions of entry into the euro, many governments on the periphery had pushed in the 1990s to bring down deficits and inflation. As they did that, they were able to borrow money more and more cheaply. Once countries joined the euro, European bank regulators started treating bonds of all eurozone governments equally; according to the officials, Greek bonds were exactly as safe as German bonds.

By the early 2000s, when everyone started using the euro, interest rates had converged completely. Plotted on a graph, the coming of the euro looks like a miracle.

It wasn't just that borrowing costs had converged. Some of the countries on the periphery of Europe were catching up with the core economically. Greece, Spain, and Ireland all saw faster-than-average economic growth for the first several years of the new cen-

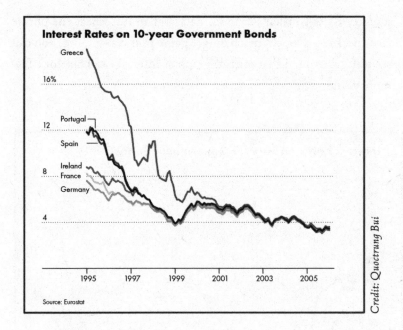

Interest Rates on 10-year Government Bonds

Greece

16%

Portugal

12

Spain

Ireland

8

France

Germany

4

1995   1997   1999   2001   2003   2005

Source: Eurostat

Credit: Quoctrung Bui

tury. The eurozone wasn't yet a single, integrated economy, but it was headed in the right direction. At least, that's how it felt at the time.

The Euro Is a Trap!

In October 2009, Greece's new prime minister stood before the country's parliament and said the Greek government had been telling a massive lie about the amount of money the Greek government was borrowing and spending. The country's deficit wasn't 6 percent, as the previous government had said, but 12 percent.

"The game is over," the head of the group of eurozone countries said a few days later. He was just talking about the Greeks monkeying with their economic data, but in retrospect the phrase also speaks to a much, much bigger game that was ending. You can see it if you stretch that miracle graph of interest rates out for a few more years.

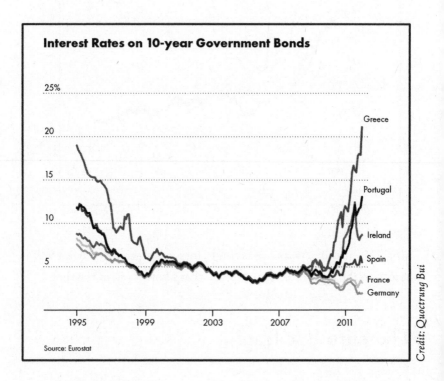

Interest Rates on 10-year Government Bonds

Source: Eurostat

Credit: Quoctrung Bui

Suddenly, nobody thought lending money to Greece was the same as lending money to Germany. Pretty soon, they started worrying about Ireland and Portugal and, eventually, Spain and Italy as well.

Rising interest rates were a potential deathtrap. In order to meet the higher interest payments, countries had to raise taxes or cut spending. This would make unemployment, which was already high, go even higher. This, in turn, would mean lower tax revenues, which would make it harder to pay off the debt.

There was a traditional way out of this trap: the central bank created money and bought government bonds on the open market. This lowered interest rates, which encouraged businesses to borrow, invest, and hire more workers, which in turn led to more tax revenues, which made it easier for the government to pay its debt. There was another benefit, as well: the lower interest rates tended to drive down the value of the currency, which made the country's exports cheaper for foreign buyers. Too much of this policy was a bad thing because it could make inflation grow out of control, but in moderation it led to more spending, more hiring, and more exports. It was the perfect solution to a financial crunch.

But Greece (and Spain and Portugal and Ireland) had given up the drachma (and the peseta and the escudo and the Irish pound). They did not have central banks to lower interest rates. They didn't have a currency to devalue. They were stuck.

So Greece asked the European Union for a bailout. In response, *Bild*, the most popular newspaper in Germany, did not cite the politicians who a few years earlier said "the common market and the euro make us strong." Instead, the paper paraphrased a new proposal from a German lawmaker: "Sell your islands, bankrupt Greeks. And the Acropolis, too!"

The narrative that took root was a classic. Countries needed bailouts because they were morally weak—especially Greece, which was in the most trouble. Countries on the periphery needed to learn the discipline of the countries in the core.

There were deep problems in Greece. Too many government employees were paid too much to do too little. As of 2010, to take one small example, there was a full-time staff of thirty people, including a full-time driver for the director, to manage the draining of a lake northwest of Athens. Reasonable enough, except for the fact that the lake was drained in 1957.

Also, almost nobody paid their taxes. One example: Greece had a luxury tax on swimming pools. In the fancy suburbs north of Athens, 324 citizens duly paid taxes on their pools. Then tax officials looked at satellite photos of the area. They counted 16,974 pools.

There was something perversely delightful about details like these. For the sensationalists in the German press, the depraved Greeks were the perfect counterparts to hardworking, willing-to-suffer-to-keep-inflation-down Germans.

But there were problems with this narrative. For one thing, it lumped Greece, where the government had borrowed too much and lied, with Spain and Ireland, where the governments had run surpluses and the problems had come from speculation in banking and real estate.

More important, the narrative omitted entirely the way in which Germany had enabled—indeed, profited from—the borrowing and spending in Greece and the other eurozone countries that suddenly found themselves in trouble. Germany's economy was driven by exports—largely by exports to other countries in the eurozone. But Germany didn't buy that much stuff from the rest of Europe. If the countries had different currencies, this imbalance would have driven up the value of the deutschmark, which would have made German exports more expensive, and Europeans would have bought less German stuff. It was only because of the euro that this didn't happen. German stuff stayed cheap because everybody was using the same money.

The money from selling all this stuff to other Europeans was piling up in Germany. What did the Germans do with all that money? They loaned it to the Southern Europeans so they could buy more stuff from Germany! German loans paid the salaries of the Greek government workers looking after the lake that didn't exist, and the Spanish construction workers building empty housing developments in La Mancha. Then those workers went out and borrowed even more German money to buy Volkswagens or, if they borrowed a lot, Mercedes.

As with the gold standard a hundred years earlier, there was a desire to tell a simple morality tale, in this case about prudent savers in Northern Europe and wasteful borrowers in Southern Europe. But as with the gold standard, the story fell apart when you looked closely at what was going on. The prudent savers and the wasteful borrowers were two sides of the same coin. "After all," the *Financial Times* columnist Martin Wolf wrote, "the borrowing would have been impossible without the lending. It is stupid to finance profligacy and then complain about the consequences of one's own choices."

It's My Money, I'll Print More If I Want To

What happened in Europe during these years was a lot like what happened in the United States in the wake of the financial crisis. And yet, as bad as the bust was in the United States, the bust was much, much worse in Europe. Europe's economy suffered more, over a longer period of time, and unemployment in Europe rose higher and took years longer to fall. The difference in outcomes explains a lot about how money works, and why it's so powerful for a country to have control over its own money.

In one way, the United States was like Southern Europe. Both were buying and borrowing from a foreign exporter. The Southern Europeans were sending euros to Germany in exchange for cars and machinery; the US was sending dollars to China in exchange for TVs and running shoes. China was lending a lot of those dollars back to the US (mostly in the form of Treasury bonds) so Americans could buy more stuff from China.

But there was a crucial difference between the US and Southern Europe: the US was borrowing in dollars, a currency China had no control over. As a result, even though the US owed China a trillion dollars (a trillion dollars!), the US had the whip hand.

After the financial crisis, the Federal Reserve launched a series of extraordinary interventions, creating trillions of new dollars out of thin air and, in the view of some critics (later shown to be wrong), threatening to drive up inflation and destroy the value of the dollar. This would also have destroyed the value of all those Treasury bonds China owned. But the Chinese had no say in US monetary policy. This is the beauty of borrowing in your own currency: it's your money, and you can print more if you want to. This is what Greece, and Portugal, and Ireland, and Spain gave up when they joined the euro.

The United States and Europe were both made up of states whose economies differed a lot from each other. Like Spain and Ireland, Florida and Nevada had booms in bank lending, home construction, and real estate prices, followed by banking crises, real estate busts, and high unemployment.

But when the unemployment rate in Nevada neared 14 percent in 2010, hundreds of millions of dollars automatically flowed into the state from the federal government in the form of unemployment insurance and food stamps. This money came from taxpayers all over the country, including places like Texas and Maine that largely avoided the boom and bust. Yet people in Texas and Maine didn't complain about bailing out wasteful Nevadans. Newspapers didn't write editorials attacking the profligate culture of Nevada and Arizona.

Americans thought about the economy as Americans, not as New Yorkers or Oregonians or whatever, and rightly so. They paid far more in taxes to the federal government than they did to their state governments, and moved frequently from state to state, often to find work. They relied on a safety net funded mostly by the federal government, and the money they saved in the bank was guaranteed by the federal government, not by the states.

None of this was true in Europe. Despite the fact that people could move freely around the eurozone for work, in practice Europeans crossed national borders much less frequently than Americans crossed state borders. The age at which workers could claim government pensions, and the generosity of those pensions, varied from country to country. (Greek workers, to take one example that proved problematic, could retire at a younger age and claim more generous pensions than German workers.) Each country had its own banking regulations and its own finance ministry.

The Europeans—at least, the ones who believed in "ever closer union"—always meant to get around to creating a unified economy, with the same rules for everyone. They knew that, for the euro to work, Europe needed to be more like a single country. "It cannot be repeated often enough: Political union is the indispensable counterpart to economic and monetary union," Chancellor Kohl had said years earlier. "Recent history, and not just that of Germany, teaches us that the idea of sustaining an economic and monetary union over time without political union is a fallacy."

Europeans had been ignoring this fallacy for years. Now it was in their faces.

In 2010, as unemployment hit 10 percent, the European Central Bank (ECB), there in Frankfurt with its Bundesbanky mission to keep prices in the euro area stable, did not create more money and lower interest rates in order to encourage businesses to borrow money and start hiring. Then, in 2011, the bank finally acted. But it did exactly the wrong thing, just like the Fed in 1931. It raised interest rates! It made things even worse!

The ECB did collaborate with the European Commission and the International Monetary Fund when they launched a series of bailouts in Greece, Portugal, and Ireland. But the money came with rules that forced governments to cut spending and raise tax rates, which in turn drove up unemployment and hurt the economy.

Greece, Portugal, and Ireland were all pretty small compared with the EU as a whole. It was clear they could limp along more or less forever on a series of underfunded bailouts, without taking the rest of Europe down with them. But in 2011, after the ECB raised interest rates, investors started getting really nervous about Spain and Italy, which were much bigger. They started demanding higher interest rates to lend to the Spanish and Italian governments, and the higher interest rates put those governments in an even more difficult economic spot. If rates kept rising, Spain and Italy might need bailouts, too—or they might be forced to crash out of the euro and go back to their old currencies, which would cause economic chaos.

The problem with Greece and Portugal had been a problem of political will; Europe and the IMF had enough money to bail out those countries. Spain and Italy were something else, though. Their combined government debts were over a trillion euros, far more than the EU and the IMF could credibly guarantee. They were so much that, in order to guarantee them, you would literally need the power to print money out of thin air.

Fortunately for Europe, there was an institution that could do that: the European Central Bank. The solution was to go back to Walter Bagehot's nineteenth-century call for the central bank to lend into a panic. Rising interest rates were a self-fulfilling prophecy that could lead to economic collapse. Europe needed a central bank willing to act as lender of last resort—to prevent panic by buying up the bonds of troubled governments.

Whatever It Takes

In 2011, an Italian economist named Mario Draghi took over as head of the ECB. He had been orphaned at fifteen and left to care for his younger siblings, studied for his PhD at MIT alongside Ben Bernanke, and been Italy's finance minister through eleven different governments in ten years. He had the personal, intellectual, and political chops for the job.

Draghi cut interest rates on his third day running the ECB, and cut them again a month later. The cuts helped, but they weren't enough. In June 2012, Spain's borrowing costs spiked to their highest level since the country had joined the euro. Italy's borrowing costs were rising as well.

"The future of the European Union will be played out in the next few days, perhaps in the coming hours," the Spanish foreign minister said. He wanted the Germans to be scared, so he added: "If the Titanic sinks, it takes everyone with it, even those travelling in first class."

The next month, Draghi was scheduled to speak on a panel in

London. It was no big deal; Draghi was in town to watch the Olympic opening ceremonies the next day. "No one had planned this to be an event of great significance," another central banker who was on the panel said later. Just before the event, Draghi said to the other panelists: "Why don't you take as much time as you want? I don't want to say much."

In the end, Draghi did not say much. But in the few minutes that he did speak, he said three words that changed the course of the euro crisis. For as long as Draghi is remembered at all, he will be remembered for those three words: "whatever it takes."

"Within our mandate," Draghi said, "the ECB is ready to do whatever it takes to preserve the euro." Pause. "And believe me, it will be enough."

That was it! Almost immediately, borrowing costs for Spain and Italy started falling. And they kept falling. Soon after that, Draghi expanded on his promise. The ECB announced a new program that allowed it to start buying the bonds of eurozone governments if there was a massive sell-off. The ECB did not actually have to buy the bonds through that program. The mere promise was enough to end the panic. Borrowing costs kept falling. The crisis was over.

In the twenty-first century, it has become wildly clear that one of the most important things central bankers do is make promises that people believe. Draghi's "whatever it takes" promise was meaningful not because it was followed by some bold action; the statement itself was the bold action. The people who were betting against the euro by dumping Spanish and Italian bonds suddenly saw that they were betting against a man who had the power to print unlimited euros to buy up those bonds—and who now said he was willing to do so. By promising to save the euro, Draghi saved the euro. That's the magic trick! Money is trust; in the modern world, where central banks have the ultimate power over money, money is trust in central bankers.

Mario Draghi swooping in to save the euro is the happy ending. The unhappy ending is this:

A new kind of money that was born out of some combination of hope (for a united Europe) and fear (of a united Germany) had taken away the sovereignty of democratic countries that were home to hundreds of millions of people. Their money, and therefore their fate, was now in the hands of foreign central bankers.

CHAPTER 15

The Radical Dream of Digital Cash

Cash is a beautiful technology. It lets me walk up to a stranger, hand over a few pieces of paper, and walk away with an armload of stuff. The stranger doesn't have to know anything about me. I don't have to know anything about her. Nobody else has to know anything about our exchange. And we don't need any record of the transaction. The cash itself is the record.

Most money doesn't work like this. The money in my checking account is just a number next to my name on the bank's digital ledger. When I buy something with my debit card or pay a bill on my phone, a new entry is added to the ledger. Indeed, the new entry in the ledger (along with the corresponding entry in the ledger of the business that is getting paid) *is the payment*. No matter what the bank tells me, this is not a fundamentally private transaction. Maybe nobody will find out about it. Or maybe I'll wind up in court, for one reason or another, forced by a government prosecutor or a disgruntled partner to disclose the checks I've written and the online payments I've made. Almost certainly, multiple companies—Amazon, Visa, Chase—are piecing together parts of my ledger to figure out every single thing there is to know about me.

In the early 1980s, a computer scientist named David Chaum saw that the rise of cheap, powerful, networked computers was about to cause a huge shift away from anonymous, untraceable cash, and toward trackable ledger money. He was terrified and thought everybody else should be, too. "The foundation is being laid for a dossier society in which computers could be used to infer individuals' life-styles, habits, whereabouts, and associations from data collected in ordinary consumer transactions," he wrote in an absurdly prescient article in a journal published by the Association for Computing Machinery. "Some of our basic liberties may be threatened by computerization under the current approach."

Chaum wasn't just some hippie-ish Cassandra complaining about technology. I mean, he was those things—he had a ponytail, and a VW bus, and he hung out in Berkeley. But he wasn't *just* those things. He also had a PhD in computer science from Berkeley and was a world expert in cryptography (the study of secret codes!) and security. And after years of technical work, he believed he had invented a new system that would let people live in the digital world without giving up their privacy. He had found a way to escape the tyranny of the bank ledger.

In a technical article subtitled "Transaction Systems to Make Big Brother Obsolete," Chaum laid out a whole new way of being in the electronic world—a new way of communicating, identifying yourself, and, most important, a new way of buying stuff. He invented digital cash.

In the decades that followed, some of the biggest corporations on the planet—Microsoft, Citibank—would be drawn to Chaum. At the same time, a small group of radical libertarian programmers also got interested in his ideas, which they thought would help create a stateless online paradise.

The giant corporations would spend millions of dollars in their quest to create proprietary digital cash. The radical programmers would work for free, often in their spare time, and would give their code away to anyone who wanted it. The corporations would ultimately fail; the radical programmers would succeed.

When Digital Cash Was the New New Thing

In 1989, after a decade in academia, David Chaum decided to save privacy or get rich trying. He took the patents he'd accumulated over the previous decade ("a device which will assist in the performance of a financial transaction, yet secure the transactions details against covert inspection") and started a company called DigiCash.

A generation before the iPhone was invented, at a moment when most people had never heard of the internet, Chaum imagined a world where you would carry around a little computer the size of a credit card. You would transfer cash from your bank account to your card—it would be just like withdrawing paper money. Stores would have card readers, to transfer cash from your account to theirs. The store's computer would talk to the bank's computer to verify that the electronic money was valid. But—and this is the clever part—Chaum figured out a system where the bank could verify the digital money without knowing the identity of the person using the money. You could buy stuff but stay out of Big Brother's ledger. It was digital, anonymous money.

Over the next few years, everybody suddenly decided digital cash was the next big thing. "Is e-money really going to happen? Inevitably," *Wired* magazine inevitably wrote. "Hard currency has been a useful item for a few millennia or so, but now it has simply worn out its welcome."

"Cash is dying," the *New York Times Magazine* said. "So here come Bitbux, E-Cash, Netchex, Cybercash, Netbills and Digicash, through the Patent and Trademark Office and into the marketplace."

Microsoft is rumored to have offered Chaum millions to integrate DigiCash into Windows. Chaum turned the company down. Citibank visited Chaum, then worked for years on its own Electronic Monetary System. It was to be a new, digital currency, issued by the bank. The federal government tested it in secret for several years, including a pilot program in which government officials used Citi's e-money to buy tens of thousands of Dell computers and collected taxes from a tobacco company—some $350 million in transactions.

Alan Greenspan, the Fed chairman who loved to warn against excessive regulation of everything, warned against excessive regulation of digital cash. "I am especially concerned that we not attempt to impede unduly our newest innovation, electronic money," he said. (Much later, after the financial crisis, Greenspan would say that he had warned against regulation too much.)

In 1994, Tim Berners-Lee, who invented the Web, invited Chaum to open the "First International Conference on the World Wide Web" in Geneva. By the end of 1995, DigiCash was working with banks in the United States, Switzerland, Germany, Australia, and Japan.

The technology was in place. Massive financial institutions were behind it. All DigiCash needed was for people to use it.

But despite what ordinary people said when you asked them about privacy ("We're for it!"), people's actions revealed they didn't really care all that much about privacy. As people started buying stuff online, they didn't bother with private digital cash. Instead, they used their credit cards. Eminently traceable, completely not secret, subject to significant fees. Also profoundly convenient.

Citibank never rolled out its Electronic Money System to the public. DigiCash went bankrupt in 1997. Bitbux, Netchex, and Cybercash were never heard from again. "Electronic money has thus turned out to be a solution in search of a problem," the *Economist* wrote in 1998 under the headline "Keep the Change."

But even as the corporate version of digital cash was dying, a loose group of libertarian programmers was using Chaum's ideas as the core of a much more radical vision. They imagined a digital cash that wouldn't just replace paper money; it would be better. They imagined a new kind of digital money that gave you all of the anonymity of cash, but with none of the constraints of paper and coins that have to be moved from place to place in the physical world. They realized digital cash could create a stateless libertarian paradise.

Techno-Libertarians of the World, Unite!

Timothy May was a physicist and engineer who retired from Intel in 1986 at age thirty-four, bought a house outside Santa Cruz, and spent his days walking on the beach and reading like it was his job. He read science fiction and he read philosophy and he read lots of technical journals, and then one day he read David Chaum's "Transaction Systems to Make Big Brother Obsolete," and it changed his life—and, maybe, the history of money—forever. "This is it," he thought. "This is the future."

May was primed to have his mind blown by Chaum's promise of digital cash. As an engineer, a libertarian, and a sci-fi fan, he grasped the technical details, the personal stakes, and the potential for profound social transformation. Indeed, his vision went even further than Chaum's. So May did what you do when you've just discovered the thing that's going to change the world and you don't have a job and you're living alone with a cat named Nietzsche: he wrote a manifesto.

"A specter is haunting the modern world," he began, allusive guns blazing, "the specter of crypto anarchy."

May's views were radical. He didn't think taxes were too high. He opposed the very idea of taxes. He opposed democracy and resented the "clueless 95 percent" of society. The undermining of the US government sounded good to him. "The Crypto Anarchist Manifesto"—wonky, grandiose, and a little bit tongue in cheek—was a call to like-minded radicals.

> Two persons may exchange messages, conduct business, and negotiate electronic contracts without ever knowing the True Name, or legal identity, of the other. Interactions over networks will be untraceable.... These developments will alter completely the nature of government regulation, [and] the ability to tax and control economic interactions...
>
> The State will of course try to slow or halt the spread of this technology, citing national security concerns, use of the technology by drug dealers and tax evaders, and fears of societal disintegration. Many of these concerns will be valid; crypto anarchy will allow national secrets to be trade freely and will allow illicit and stolen materials to be traded....But this will not halt the spread of crypto anarchy...

Weirdly, the manifesto worked.

Not immediately, though. When May handed out photocopies at a cryptography event Chaum was hosting in Santa Barbara in 1988, nobody seemed interested. But over the next few years, a community of libertarian coders started to coalesce around May and his manifesto.

In 1992, they got together at a house in Oakland. The house had just been bought by a mathematician named Eric Hughes, who was back from a stint working for Chaum in the Netherlands. At the gathering, everybody sat on the floor because Hughes hadn't bought furniture yet. May opened the party by reading his manifesto. The crowd loved it. They played a cryptography game and had Thai food for dinner. People crashed on the floor.

One of the people at the party, a journalist named Jude Milhon, thought the group needed a snappier, less scary-sounding name than "crypto anarchists." She called them the cypherpunks. Like cyberpunks, but really into codes—cyphers.

The cypherpunks offered a broader tent than the crypto anarchists. And, crucially for our story, they weren't just into philosophy. They wanted to write the code that would create the money that would change the world.

"Privacy in an open society requires anonymous transaction systems. Until now, cash has been the primary such system," Eric Hughes wrote in 1992 in (wait for it) yet another manifesto. *A Cypherpunk's Manifesto* was less grandiose and more focused than May's manifesto. It was less of a declaration for the history books, more of a call to get to work.

We the Cypherpunks are dedicated to building anonymous systems. We are defending our privacy with cryptography, with anonymous mail forwarding systems, with digital signatures, and with electronic money ...

Cypherpunks write code.... Our code is free for all to use, world-wide. We don't much care if you don't approve of the software we write. We know that software can't be destroyed and that a widely dispersed system can't be shut down ...

The Cypherpunks are actively engaged in making the networks safer for privacy. Let us proceed together apace.

Onward.

Inventing Digital, Anonymous Cash Is Really Hard

What the cypherpunks needed, out there on the virtual barricades of the digital revolution, was a kind of untraceable electronic cash that didn't force them to trust a corporation like DigiCash, much less Microsoft or (God forbid) Citibank. What they needed was a kind of digital money that didn't require them to trust anyone at all. They needed to be able to trust the money itself. Just like gold.

But this was a really hard thing to create. In the case of simple paper money, it hadn't been easy. In that thousand-year-old paper bill from China, half of the space was given over to a warning that counterfeiting was punishable by death. And that bill itself was probably a counterfeit! The cypherpunks' digital cash wouldn't have the threat of state violence to scare counterfeiters away. And most ordinary digital files can be counterfeited by anyone who can type ctrl-c, ctrl-v.

It was an extraordinarily hard technical problem. And yet, true to the manifesto ("cypherpunks write code"), cypherpunks started writing the code.

The first breakthrough came five years after that initial cypherpunk meeting, from a British professor named Adam Back. He was trying to solve a problem that was driving everybody crazy back in the mid-'90s: email spam.

The cypherpunks used software that allowed them to send email anonymously. But that same software was catnip for spammers, who used it to send millions of unblockable junk emails. In 1997, Back emailed the cypherpunk list to share a program he'd written that "would put spammers out of business overnight."

A few years earlier, two computer scientists named Cynthia Dwork and Moni Naor had published a paper called "Pricing via Processing, or Combatting Junk Mail." The basic idea was to require computers to do a tiny bit of computational work before sending an email. The work might take a few seconds—short enough to be irrelevant for ordinary people, but long enough to destroy the business model of spammers who had been sending thousands of emails per minute.

Back put this idea into practice by requiring computers sending emails to perform a type of computation called a "hash." In Back's system, coming up with the right hash was hard—the email sender's computer had to do a lot of work. But once the answer had been discovered, it was easy for another computer to verify that it was correct. So Back made the email sender's computer do the hard computational work and add the solution to the outgoing email. Then the recipient's computer verified that the hash was correct. Back called the program hashcash. Versions of hashcash were adopted by a bunch of anti-spam software programs, including one released by Microsoft.

Hashcash solved problem number one for creating digital money: how to prevent computers from creating infinite amounts of money.

David Chaum had first taken a crack at the problem by relying on a central institution, such as a bank. But the cypherpunks' dream was to embed scarcity in digital money itself so that buyers and sellers wouldn't need to trust any central institution. Back's proposal was an elegant solution. Anyone who wanted hashcash had to put in some computational work to get it. The cost of the electricity to power that computation, tiny as it might seem, created scarcity.

Chaum's digital money was like fiat currency, controlled by a central bank. Back's was more like gold, at least in one respect: just as anyone with the resources and the will could mine gold, anyone with the resources and the will could create hashcash.

But there was also an essential way in which hashcash was not like gold—a way in which it wouldn't work as the digital money the coders needed to make their cypherpunk dreams come true. Each hashcash "postage stamp" was customized for a particular email recipient and could only be used once. So it wouldn't work as money.

✴ ✴ ✴

The cypherpunks were up against what felt like a paradox. To create digital money they had to prevent someone from spending the same money twice, or three times, or a hundred times. The classic way to do this was by keeping track of everyone's balance on a ledger. They could make the ledger anonymous to protect users' privacy— that was what Chaum had done. But they still needed some trusted intermediary to maintain the ledger, to keep track of everything.

In 1998, a coder named Wei Dai suggested an upside-down solution. Maybe we don't need a single, central intermediary to maintain the ledger. Maybe we make *everybody* maintain the ledger. The way to create anonymous digital money is for everybody to know everything all the time—every balance, every payment, at every moment. "Every participant maintains a (separate) database of how much money belongs to each pseudonym," Dai wrote. "These accounts collectively define the ownership of money." Dai called it b-money.

As in hashcash, computers would generate b-money by solving puzzles. When a computer belonging to a user—call her Alice—solved a puzzle, the computer would send the answer to everyone on the network. Everyone would verify the answer, and credit Alice's account in the ledger with newly created b-money.

And if Alice wants to pay someone—call him Bob—five b-money bucks, Alice sends a message to the computers of everyone who uses b-money: "I, Alice, am paying Bob five bucks." Everybody's computer first checks to make sure that Alice has at least five bucks in her account. If she doesn't, her message is ignored. If she does, then everybody's computer deducts five bucks from Alice's account and adds five bucks to Bob's account. And the payment is made. (For anonymity, people's accounts are not listed in their own names, but in codes of letters and numbers.)

It was beautiful, but there was a flaw, and it was obvious to Dai from the start. The system was "impractical, because it makes heavy use of a synchronous and unjammable anonymous broadcast channel." In other words, everybody has to be online all the time communicating to each other instantaneously and without interruption. Otherwise, somebody could miss a transaction sent out across the network and then the ledgers wouldn't match, so you couldn't figure out who had how much money.

The cypherpunks kicked Dai's idea around. A few of them built on it. One guy described a system called "bit gold"; another wrote code for what he called "reusable proofs of work," which built off hashcash.

Then, in August 2008, Wei Dai got an email from a stranger. "I was very interested to read your b-money page," it began. "I'm getting ready to release a paper that expands on your ideas into a complete working system. Adam Back (hashcash.org) noticed the similarities and pointed me to your site."

The paper's working title, included in the email to Dai, was "Electronic Cash Without a Trusted Third Party." Two months later, the stranger published the paper online with an updated title. It was called "Bitcoin: A Peer-to-Peer Electronic Cash System."

Bitcoin!

The stranger who invented bitcoin was almost certainly not named Satoshi Nakamoto, but that was the name on the top of the bitcoin paper, and the name in the email to Wei Dai, and the name the creator (or creators) of bitcoin used to talk up bitcoin on the crypto email lists. Nobody knew then, and nobody knows as I write this, who Satoshi Nakamoto is (or are) or was (or were).

Satoshi Nakamoto could be a cypherpunk living in an underground bunker in New Zealand or an executive at a bank in London. She might be a priest or he might be a criminal or they might be a cabal scheming to take over the world. But fundamental to the genius of bitcoin is this: it doesn't matter at all who Satoshi Nakamoto is.

It would be catastrophic if the CEO of a bank was delusional, or the chairman of the Federal Reserve was inclined to commit fraud. Those institutions depend on the choices made by the people in charge. The point of bitcoin is that no one is in charge. (You could also say that everyone is in charge, but that amounts to the same thing.) In classic cypherpunk style, Satoshi ("Satoshi") owns no patents on bitcoin. The full codebase was published online for everyone to see and use and tweak however they want.

Money is always and everywhere based on trust. Modern currency is based on trust in the government that issues it. Bitcoin is also based on trust. But the dream of bitcoin is that you don't have to trust a government, or a bank, or Satoshi Nakamoto; you just have to trust the code.

And the code for bitcoin is very clever! Satoshi took ideas from Back's hashcash and Wei Dai's b-money and added to them a few brilliant twists that seemed to make bitcoin the thing cypherpunks had been dreaming of for years: an anonymous(ish), money(ish) thing that buyers and sellers could exchange over the internet without any bank or tech company in the middle. Satoshi laid out the whole thing in that nine-page paper he published on Halloween 2008.

Bitcoin would run on a ledger maintained by everyone. When Alice wanted to give Bob five bitcoins, she would send a message to everyone, as with b-money, using her pseudonymous private key, saying: "Dear Everyone, I'm giving Bob five bitcoins." Then everyone on the network would update their universal ledger and move the bitcoins into Bob's account.

This was the system that Wei Dai had thought up—and rejected as impractical because it required everybody to keep their computers running and connected to each other and processing this giant ledger all the time. Why would anybody want to do that? Satoshi's answer to that question is maybe the most important innovation in bitcoin: the computers that were running and talking to each other and keeping track of the bitcoin ledger would get paid in newly created bitcoin for doing that work.

It works like this:

- Every new transaction gets broadcast out to the network.

- All the computers in the network are recording those transactions and, at the same time, trying to solve a computational puzzle. (The puzzle-solving idea goes back to Adam Back's hashcash.)

- The first computer to solve the puzzle sends the solution, along with a record of the most recent transactions on the ledger, out to all the computers on the network. This record of transactions is known as a block.

- The computers on the network check to confirm that the solution to the puzzle is correct. Once they see that it is, they begin again, recording new transactions in a new block and trying to solve the next computational puzzle.

- Each block of transactions is linked to the block that came before. In this way, all transactions in the history of bitcoin are linked together forever. In the white paper, Satoshi called this a "chain of blocks." It would soon get the slightly shorter, significantly snappier name "blockchain."

In early 2009, Satoshi published the source code for bitcoin. Anyone who wanted to, anywhere in the world, could download the code to their computer and start solving computational puzzles, packaging blocks of transactions, and winning bitcoin.

The winner for each block would get 50 bitcoins—which, at the time, was worth nothing at all. But at least, at the beginning, it was easy to win. "I made the proof-of-work difficulty ridiculously easy to start with, so for a little while in the beginning a typical PC will be able to generate coins in just a few hours," Satoshi wrote in an early email to a crypto group. If more people joined the network, the difficulty would rise so that, no matter how many computers were on the bitcoin network trying to solve problems, a new block of transactions would be created every 10 minutes.

Like gold, the amount of bitcoins that would ever exist in the world would be finite—21 million in total. They would be awarded according to a strict schedule written into the code. For the first four years, the winner for each block would get 50 bitcoins. For the four years after that, the prize would go down to 25 bitcoins per block. It would be halved every four years, down into fractions of bitcoins, until finally, in the year 2140, the last fraction of the 21 millionth bitcoin would be created. "When that runs out," Satoshi wrote, "the system can support transaction fees if needed." Satoshi was already taking a very long view.

Just before the bitcoin code was released, Satoshi had created the first block of bitcoin. With perhaps a bit more drama than is absolutely necessary, it came to be called the "genesis block," and it contained a little extra text: a front-page headline from the *Times of London* from January 3, 2009. It has been suggested that this was to prove that the genesis block was created on or after that date, in the same way a kidnapping victim is photographed holding up today's newspaper to prove he's still alive. But the choice of this particular headline, from this particular newspaper, conveys more than just the date:

```
00000070 00 00 00 00 00 00 FF FF FF FF 4D 04 FF FF 00 1D......ÿÿÿÿM.ÿÿ..
00000080 01 04 45 54 68 65 20 54 69 6D 65 73 20 30 33 2F ..EThe Times 03/
00000090 4A 61 6E 2F 32 30 30 39 20 43 68 61 6E 63 65 6C Jan/2009 Chancel
000000A0 6C 6F 72 20 6F 6E 20 62 72 69 6E 6B 20 6F 66 20 lor on brink of
```

000000B0 73 65 63 6F 6E 64 20 62 61 69 6C 6F 75 74 20 66 **second bailout f**
000000C0 6F 72 20 62 61 6E 6B 73 FF FF FF FF 01 00 F2 05 **or banks**ÿÿÿÿ..ò.
000000D0 2A 01 00 00 00 43 41 04 67 8A FD B0 FE 55 48 27 *....CA.gŠÿ°þUH′

Bitcoin was a real technical advance. It solved a set of problems that had vexed really smart people for twenty years, and it allowed for digital cash without a trusted intermediary. But bitcoin also benefited from arriving on the scene in the middle of the financial crisis, a moment when hundreds of millions of people who had never paid much attention to the meaning of money suddenly found themselves much less trustful of trusted intermediaries.

"The root problem with conventional currency is all the trust that's required to make it work," Satoshi wrote to a message board in February 2009. "The central bank must be trusted not to debase the currency, but the history of fiat currencies is full of breaches of that trust. Banks must be trusted to hold our money and transfer it electronically, but they lend it out in waves of credit bubbles with barely a fraction in reserve. We have to trust them with our privacy, trust them not to let identity thieves drain our accounts."

At a moment when trust was at a low point, bitcoin seemed to solve the problem of trusting other people to make money work. All you had to do was trust the code. But in the end, bitcoin would prove as dependent on the messiness of humans as every other kind of money.

How Much Is One Bitcoin Worth?

When you have a new kind of money, and it's not convertible at a fixed rate to dollars, or to gold, or to anything else, how much is that new kind of money worth? There are two obvious answers:

1. Whatever people will pay for it

2. Nothing

If you want to be pedantic about it, you could say that number 2 is a subset of number 1, but in any case, number 2 is what prevailed with bitcoin for kind of a long time. In 2010, more than a year after the first bitcoins were created, the coder and early bitcoin supporter Gavin Andresen created a site he called "bitcoin faucet" that gave people five bitcoins for free, just for showing up at the site and setting up their own bitcoin address. "No catch—I want Bitcoin to be successful, so I created this little service to give you a few coins to start with," Gavin wrote on the site.

Around the same time, a guy in Jacksonville, Florida, named Laszlo Hanyecz decided it was time for someone, somewhere on planet Earth, to do with bitcoin what you are supposed to do with money: buy something. So he did the obvious thing. He posted a note to the main bitcoin forum at 12:35 in the morning under the subject line "Pizza for bitcoin?"

> I'll pay 10,000 bitcoins for a couple of pizzas…like maybe 2 large ones so I have some left over for the next day. I like having left over pizza to nibble on later. You can make the pizza yourself and bring it to my house or order it for me from a delivery place….If you're interested please let me know and we can work out a deal.
>
> Thanks,
> Laszlo

A few days later, a nineteen-year-old in California hit Laszlo up via internet chat. Laszlo sent him 10,000 bitcoins and the teenager called a Papa John's in Jacksonville and ordered two pizzas with everything to be delivered to Laszlo's house (he paid with a credit card). How much was bitcoin worth at this point? Figure $30 worth of pizza for 10,000 bitcoins, which means each bitcoin was worth a third of a cent. It rounds down to nothing.

This was obviously a stunt, and to call those pizzas the first thing ever bought with bitcoin seems sort of iffy, but I want to give it to Laszlo. It's a fun stunt, and it captures the spirit of a particular bitcoin moment in its lightness and hope and silliness and insiderness. The guys in the AV club were setting up the PA system, tapping the mic, and singing goofy songs to each other in an empty room. "Is this thing on?"

The show was about to start for real. People were about to start buying stuff with bitcoin, and the scene was about to get darker. It was the kind of thing the cypherpunks had been dreaming of for twenty years—and it was brought to life by a true believer from a new generation.

Bitcoin Gets Dark

"For years I was frustrated and defeated by what seemed to be insurmountable barriers between the world today and the world I wanted," someone calling himself the Dread Pirate Roberts wrote in 2012. It was a typical sentiment for a thoughtful twentysomething struggling to find a place in the world, which is what the Dread Pirate had been—until he discovered his purpose.

"But eventually I found something I could agree with whole

heartedly. Something that made sense, was simple, elegant, and consistent in all cases." What he had found was a thread of radical libertarianism called anarcho-capitalism that held that the market was freedom, and government was tyranny. The noble thing to do, Roberts decided, was to fight tyranny by doing business on the black market.

Dread Pirate Roberts realized that his purpose in life was to start a website where people could buy drugs. And he quickly saw that bitcoin—pseudonymous digital cash—was the way to make it work.

He called the site Silk Road. It was a marketplace that matched buyers and sellers (aka dealers) of everything illegal to put in your body: weed, ecstasy, opioids, psychedelics, whatever. Listings had a Craigslist vibe, only druggier:

"5gr UNCUT Crystal Cocaine!!"

"HIGH QUALITY #4 HEROIN ALL ROCK."

In at least one way, money is like anything else: when demand increases faster than supply, the price goes up. Now that people had a reason to want bitcoin, the price of bitcoin relative to dollars started to rise. By early 2011, you could exchange one dollar for one bitcoin. After the website Gawker published the first mainstream story about Silk Road in June, the exchange rate spiked to more than $30 per bitcoin.

In 2013, the FBI arrested a man named Ross Ulbricht, who they said was the Dread Pirate Roberts, the creator of Silk Road. Ulbricht was tried and found guilty of drug trafficking and conspiracy to commit money laundering. "The stated purpose [of Silk Road] was to be beyond the law," the judge said at Ulbricht's sentencing. "In the world you created over time, democracy didn't exist." She gave him life in prison without parole.

Anarcho-Capitalism, But Without the Anarchy

In 2013, just a month after Ulbricht was arrested, the Senate Committee on Homeland Security had a hearing on bitcoin. Everyone dutifully cited all the bad things people were doing with bitcoin. And then, sort of shockingly, the mood in the room changed. A Justice Department lawyer testified that there were "many legitimate uses" of bitcoin. "These virtual currencies are not in and of themselves illegal," he said. A Treasury Department official who dealt with financial crime sounded more like a bland venture capitalist. "Innovation is a very important part of our economy," she said. *The Washington Post* called it a "love fest."

What was going on?

Silicon Valley had started to seize on bitcoin as the next big thing. There was less bitcoiny talk about ending the tyranny of democracy and more about offering lower transaction fees for online purchases. "The appeal of zero transaction costs is really strong and extremely disruptive for a massive industry, the payments industry," a venture capitalist told the *Wall Street Journal* in May 2013. ("Extremely disruptive" and "massive industry" are venture-capital speak for "there are boatloads of money to be made here.")

This view lacked the world-historical punch of the crypto anarchist manifesto, but it was very exciting to rich people seeking to become more rich. Also, lower transaction fees would be good for everybody except the payments companies currently collecting high transaction fees. Millions of dollars in venture capital started flowing into start-ups that were making bitcoin wallets and bitcoin exchanges and "Buy with Bitcoin" buttons for online merchants.

It was anarcho-capitalism, but without the anarchy. Bitcoin, weirdly, had become sort of normal. As it became clear bitcoin was legit, and wasn't about to get shut down or disappear, more people began exchanging dollars for bitcoin. The exchange rate between dollars and bitcoin shot up to over $500 around the time of the Senate hearing.

People started building special computers optimized to mine bitcoin—to attack the problems that the bitcoin software used to award new bitcoins. Then they started filling giant warehouses full of racks of those mining computers. The computers sucked up so much energy that miners began seeking out places in the world where power was cheap, to lower their costs of mining. Vast mining operations sprung up in Iceland, Mongolia, and, especially, China.

All this growth led to a new problem. Actually an old problem, now newly urgent. The bitcoin network could only process about five transactions per second. The Visa network, by comparison can process 24,000 transactions per second. This was not a technology that was about to become the new world currency.

Bitcoin was, among other things, a piece of software—lines of code, written in the programming language C++, that anyone in the world could download and do whatever they wanted with. Like all software, bitcoin would need to be tweaked over time. And a fairly straightforward tweak would have solved the transaction limit problem, by allowing each block to include more transactions.

But as with many tweaks, there would be a trade-off. The larger block size would make it harder for ordinary people to download and run bitcoin software, pushing bitcoin further away from the decentralized, egalitarian ideal and more toward a corporate, consolidated future. Was the trade-off worth it?

If bitcoin were run by a company, the CEO would have had some meetings, talked to customers, weighed the costs and benefits, and decided whether to make the tweak. But bitcoin is not run by a company. There is no CEO. The whole point is that nobody is in charge. So who decides what changes to make? Everybody!

Bitcoin is democratic. The official blockchain is whatever most of the computer processors mining bitcoins say it is. On top of that, anyone who wants to can take the bitcoin code, tweak it, and create their own, new and improved version of bitcoin. This sounds like chaos, and it kind of is, and that was kind of the point of bitcoin all along.

The fight over increasing the transaction limit—making the bitcoin network faster but less democratic—became known as the "bitcoin civil war," and it was partly about whether and when bitcoin was really going to function as money. In one camp were people who thought the most important thing about bitcoin was that it be easy to use to buy stuff. This is a good feature for money to have! These were the people who wanted to increase the block size.

People in the other camp wanted to make sure anybody who wanted to could download and run the bitcoin software. These people talked about bitcoin more like gold—this scarce valuable thing—that we shouldn't mess with too much. And, they said, even with small blocks there would eventually be a technical solution to the transaction problem. (The idea was to build software that would sort of sit on top of the core bitcoin layer and reduce the number of transactions that needed to go through the core system.)

There were summits and meetings and agreements, then changes to the agreements, and in the end everybody sort of gave up on agreeing. The big blockers launched a rival currency, which they called bitcoin cash, that allowed for far more transactions per second than bitcoin. The small blockers stuck with bitcoin. Everybody stayed mad at everybody else. They never worked it out.

Over these same years, people launched hundreds of alternative cryptocurrencies. They all ran on blockchains but had their own tweaks. They promised better anonymity or a stable value relative to the dollar. They promised whole new kinds of businesses built on top of the blockchain. Some of these coins developed huge followings and billion-dollar valuations. Most failed and became known as shitcoins.

Eventually, the Chinese government started developing its own digital currency. In other words, a technology originally conceived to "make Big Brother obsolete" was now being advanced by a state built on surveillance of its citizens.

This new universe was expanding, but bitcoin remained at the center, far more valuable than any other cryptocurrency.

"I used to think that bitcoin was just 'Trust the math, trust the code,'" Gavin Andresen, the coder and early bitcoin evangelist told me. "My mind has changed about that. There is a community. There is consensus. There are people."

Andresen—the first person Satoshi handed the code to, who gave away thousands of bitcoins because he believed so much in the process—eventually got so tired of the bitcoin civil war that he left the bitcoin world altogether. (For the record, in the bitcoin civil war, Andresen believed in bigger blocks.)

The Price of Bitcoin

As the nerds were fighting over the future of bitcoin, the exchange rate between bitcoins and dollars rose, then it rose some more, then it got completely ridiculous. A little later, it fell but remained much higher than it had been. Even after the crash, you could exchange a single bitcoin for thousands of dollars.

This was generally seen as a good thing by people who were excited about bitcoin, not least because they had already exchanged dollars for bitcoins and—their belief in the inevitable failure of the dollar notwithstanding—they were excited by the future prospect of exchanging their bitcoins for many, many, many more dollars. Simply put, the people who bought bitcoin early got rich, and this made them happy about bitcoin.

And yet! For people who wanted bitcoin to be money—to be a thing ordinary people used to buy stuff because they cared about privacy, or because it was cheaper for merchants than accepting credit cards, or whatever—the wild rise in bitcoin's value was a disaster.

In 2021, for example, the exchange rate more than doubled, rising from around $30,000 per bitcoin to a peak of over $60,000. If we lived in a world where bitcoin was really money—where we got paid in bitcoin, and got mortgages in bitcoin, and bought groceries in bitcoin—this rise in the value of bitcoin would have caused a deflation far worse than the one in the Great Depression. It would have suddenly taken twice as much work to pay off a student loan or a mortgage. It would have destroyed the economy.

Then, starting in November 2021, the value of bitcoin collapsed almost in half. In a world where people used bitcoin as money, this would have meant prices nearly doubled in a few months—an inflation rate far worse than anything the United States has seen since the Revolutionary War.

Indeed, people don't even usually speak of an "exchange rate" between bitcoins and dollars. Instead, they talk about the "price of bitcoin." It's also common to multiply the price of one bitcoin by the number of bitcoins in existence and call the result bitcoin's "market cap." Nobody talks about money this way.

Supporters of bitcoin say the price rise is evidence bitcoin has become a "store of value." The phrase describes one of the traditional attributes of money. But store of value means, more or less, a thing that holds a stable value over time. If $100 buys your family a week's worth of groceries today, there is a very good chance it will buy approximately a week's worth of groceries a year from now. The dollar is a good store of value (it tends to lose about 2 percent of its value every year).

The amount of bitcoin that buys you a week's worth of groceries today might buy you only a day's groceries a year from now. Or it might buy you an entire grocery store. It is not, by any stretch, a good store of value.

What the people who say bitcoin is a store of value mean—or, at least, a more plausible thing to say—is that bitcoin has become a speculative investment. Bitcoin is a thing people buy because they think they are going to be able to sell it for more in the future—though they recognize they might have to sell it for less. This is not, in general, a useful quality in money.

The history of money is largely the history of stuff becoming money without people really realizing it. Banknotes and then bank deposits started out as a record of a debt and sort of crept their way into being full-blown money. Shadow banking grew for decades before anybody thought to call it shadow banking. It was only in moments of crisis—the moment when the thing suddenly threatened to become not-money—that everyone looked around and said, well, I guess banknotes and bank deposits and money-market mutual funds are money now.

The history of electronic money is exactly the opposite. Someone—David Chaum, Satoshi Nakamoto—has a very clever technological breakthrough. Then they climb up to the mountaintop and proclaim to the world: "Here is a new kind of money!" And then it doesn't really become money. Or at least it hasn't yet.

Conclusion: The Future
of Money

Money is a choice, or a set of choices. But it doesn't feel that way. It just feels like the way things are. Then someone has an insight. They say: We are doing money all wrong. Here's a better way to do it.

Everybody else says: What are you talking about? What we have *now* is real money. What you're talking about is just some crazy idea you made up!

Usually, that's the end of it. But once in a while, something happens—a financial crisis, or a major political shift, or some new technology, or some combination of all three of those. And then suddenly everybody starts listening to those fringy people with the strange ideas about money, and there's something new: paper money backed by gold, or paper money backed by nothing, or numbers on a computer.

There are lots of smart people who think that the way we do money right now is ridiculous, and they're confident they have a better idea for how to do things. Their ideas are useful—not only in and of themselves, but also as a reminder that there's nothing natural or inevitable about the way money works now. We know money will be very different in the future; we just don't know what kind of different it will be. Here are three possibilities.

A World Without Cash

Of all the ways that money might change, one is particularly easy to imagine: paper money might disappear. When you can use a debit card to buy a pack of gum, what's even the point of paper money?

This has been happening for a long time. Sending mobile money via text message took off in Kenya in 2007. By 2020, a single Chinese mobile payments app, called Alipay, was used by roughly 1 billion people.

But in much of the world, even as payment apps proliferate, something strange is happening. Year after year, the amount of paper money floating around keeps growing faster than the overall economy.

By 2020, there was more than $5,000 in paper dollars for every man, woman, and child in the United States. (This doesn't count cash in bank vaults; it's just money out in circulation.) The numbers are similar for the eurozone and Japan.

Where is all that money? What are people doing with it? Nobody knows! It's just pieces of paper out in the world! Some people are doubtless using hundred-dollar bills for very legal and very cool purposes. Some people in developing countries are keeping their life savings in dollar bills and euro notes to protect themselves against unreliable local currencies and shaky banks. Also, lots and lots of people are using lots and lots of cash to evade taxes and traffic in drugs, people, and stolen merchandise.

One reason we can infer this is that almost all of the cash is in big bills. There are more hundred-dollar bills than one-dollar bills! There are more than forty hundred-dollar bills out in the world for every man, woman, and child in America. More than a trillion dollars in hundreds. The obvious fact is that hundreds (and other large bills) aren't particularly useful for everyday life but are extraordinarily useful for committing crimes and for evading taxes (which is itself a crime).

Cash is less and less necessary for daily (honest) life. Since cash makes crime easier, and it's not going to disappear on its own, should governments get rid of cash to fight crime?

The case against cash has been made most compellingly by Ken Rogoff, a former chief economist at the International Monetary Fund, now at Harvard. He argues not for getting rid of money entirely, but for getting rid of big bills and maybe ultimately replacing small bills with coins. The idea is to allow small cash transactions to continue but to make big cash transactions very inconvenient, which would effectively raise the cost of using cash to commit crimes.

Rogoff also points to be another, less intuitive benefit to getting rid of paper money: it could help countries recover faster from economic crises by making it easier for central banks to set negative interest rates.

When you put money in the bank, the bank pays you interest, and your account grows a little every month. If interest rates were negative, your account would shrink a little every month. You would be paying the bank to hold your money. If this started happening, you and lots of other people might go to the bank and demand all your money in large bills and go stick it in a vault. Some central banks in Europe have set rates at a fraction of a percent below zero, but they are afraid that if they go much lower, everybody would pull their cash out of the bank. Effectively, the floor for interest rates is zero minus the cost of storing cash in a vault.

Negative rates sound awful. But in a crisis, they might make almost everybody better off. In 2009, when US businesses were frantically cutting spending and firing hundreds of thousands of workers every month, it might have been useful if the Fed could have pushed interest rates well below zero. Negative rates would have given panicked businesses an incentive to hire and invest, rather than fire and save. But in 2009 the Fed could lower its key interest rate only to zero. And because that wasn't really low enough, unemployment remained high, spending remained low, and the economy stagnated.

There is one place in the developed world where cash is disappearing already: Sweden. When I first heard this, I assumed it was because everyone in Sweden is perfect and nobody commits crimes, so they don't need cash; but in fact it's sort of the opposite. There were a series of violent robberies in the mid-2000s, including one where a gang of thieves stole a helicopter, landed it on the roof of a cash depot, broke through a skylight with sledgehammers, blew their way into a vault, and flew away with 39 million kronor (more than $5 million). Police response was slowed by fake bombs the thieves had planted at the police helicopter station and metal spikes they'd put on the roads. A few of the thieves were caught and convicted, but almost none of the stolen money was ever recovered.

Cash use started falling quickly after that. In 2010, 39 percent of Swedes said they'd used cash for their most recent purchase; that fell to 13 percent in 2018. Around half the bank branches in the country stopped allowing cash withdrawals or cash deposits. The bank didn't want your money. Instead, they encouraged people to use cards or a payment app called Swish. This provoked a polite backlash from some quarters. "We aren't against the digital movement, but we think it's going a bit too fast," the president of the Swedish National Pensioners' Association said.

In 2019, the Swedes passed a law that required many bank branches to carry cash. (You now need a law to force banks to carry cash!) And the Riksbank—the central bank that four hundred years earlier had created the first state-authorized paper money in Europe—was trying to figure out how to issue e-krona, a digital currency that people could use through accounts at the central bank, or through rechargeable payment cards.

Maybe the most striking thing about the disappearance of cash is that we may not really care—sort of like what's already happening with personal checks. If cash disappears, it will be harder to commit petty tax evasion, and the surveillance economy will intrude on us more than ever. The government will need to provide subsidized debit cards for people who don't have bank accounts. But already, today, most money is not paper or coins. It's money people have in their bank accounts. The core of money today isn't pieces of paper. It's bank deposits. It's numbers stored on bank computers. That's what money is, and has been, for decades.

Cash could disappear, but our basic way of creating and managing money—with central banks, and commercial banks, and shadow banks—would remain unchanged. A much bigger change would come from getting rid of banks as we know them—an idea that has been backed by a surprising number of really smart people, for a long time.

A World Without Banks

Most of the money in the world is not just stored in private banks; it is created by private banks. When banks make loans, the proceeds are ultimately deposited in someone's bank account as more money.

For nearly a hundred years, some of the smartest economists in every generation have said this is a horrible way to do money. It started in the 1930s when a group of the most famous economists in America (including our man Irving Fisher) wrote that banks' ability to create and destroy money was "a chief loose screw in our present American money and banking system." Their solution: the government should end banking as we know it.

A government ban on banks sounds like a lefty dream. But lots of economists who love the free market and are wary of government intervention have argued for forcing private banks out of the business of creating money. Milton Friedman, whose crusade for free markets inspired Ronald Reagan and Margaret Thatcher, suggested ending banking as we know it. John Cochrane, a contemporary economist at the (conservative) Hoover Institution and (libertarian) Cato Institute, has called banks a "huge, crony-capitalist nightmare."

Banks are private companies that create and destroy a public resource—money. Because money is so essential, the government offers a massive but piecemeal safety net for the banks. Central banks are lenders of last resort. Government insurance programs back deposits. Regulators from multiple agencies try to keep banks safe, but sometimes fail to do so.

When banks were bailed out after the financial crisis of 2008, people raged against "too big to fail" banks. The anger is justifiable, but the problem isn't that banks are too big or that bankers are too greedy; the problem is with the nature of banking. Banking is inherently prone to crises. And in any big financial crisis, the government has to choose between bailing out banks (whether they are big or small) or allowing failing banks to take down the whole economy.

Cochrane and Friedman and Fisher step back, look at the system, and say, Wait. Why does it have to be like this at all? The root of the issue is that basic banks do these two, very different things.

1. They hold our money and make it easier for us to get paid and make payments.

2. They make loans.

The dazzlingly simple argument from all of these great economists comes down to this: split those into separate businesses. Variations on this idea are usually called "100% reserve banking" or "full-reserve banking" (as opposed to the current, fractional-reserve banking system) or "narrow banking." The details of the plans vary, but here's a simple sketch.

In this new world, one kind of business—call it a money warehouse—would hold our money. Our paychecks would get deposited there. We could pay our bills from our account there. We could get cash from the money warehouse's ATMs. The money warehouse would store our money in an account at the Federal Reserve. We might pay a small fee to keep our money at the money warehouse. Fair enough. It's a useful service!

A different kind of business—call it a lender—would make loans. The money for those loans would come from investors' money, and the investors would be prepared to lose that money if the loans didn't get paid back. There are already mutual funds that work like this. They take investors' money and buy corporate bonds, which is a way of lending money to corporations. If the corporations don't pay the money back, the investors take a loss. In a world without banks, you could have something like mutual funds make the loans that banks used to make.

In this world, there is no such thing as a bank run. If everyone who had their money at the money warehouse suddenly asked for their money back, the warehouse would say: Okay, here you go. And everybody would get their money back.

It's hard to overstate how big of a change this would be. We would no longer need deposit insurance. We would no longer need a lender of last resort. We would no longer need thousands of pages of rules that are supposed to keep banks safe. Money warehouses and lenders could not start booms by creating money; even more important, they could not crash the economy by going bust and destroying money. Beautiful.

Think about it too hard, and two problems emerge. First, there will always be people who want to park their money somewhere and get paid some interest, people who are looking to borrow, and profit-seeking matchmakers. People will keep reinventing shadow banking. This is a big problem when shadow banking gets big, as it did in the early 2000s, but it is potentially solvable with the right set of rules. Potentially.

The second problem is weirder and more interesting. If all we did was ban banks from taking deposits and lending money, a vast amount of money would disappear. If we stop banks from creating money, where is all the money going to come from? The short answer is that central banks would have to create much more money. The power dynamic of money would shift from private banks to central banks.

There was a moment, in the insanity of 1933, when a shift to the world of full-reserve banks could have happened. But instead, we wound up with the regime we still live with today—deposit insurance, the modern Federal Reserve, and banks that both take deposits and make loans. After the crisis of 2008, the head of the Bank of England said, "Of all the many ways of organizing banking, the worst is the one we have today."

But the response in Parliament in the UK, like the response in the US Congress, was to turn the dials on the system as it exists, not to fundamentally transform the system. The interests in favor of the status quo, these lawmakers found, are vast. It would take another big financial crisis to make full-reserve banking—or, for that matter, any radical change to the way we do money—a real political possibility.

A World Where the Government Prints Money and Gives It to Anybody Who Wants a Job

In early 2019, Alexandria Ocasio-Cortez, a newly elected congresswoman, started proposing massive new government projects—including a promise of a government job for any citizen who wanted one. People asked her how the government would pay for it. Maybe we'll tax the rich, she said. Or maybe, she suggested, we can just spend the money and not worry about how to pay for it. She wasn't being glib; she was drawing on a weird new way of thinking about money that had quietly been gathering steam for decades and was suddenly everywhere (or at least everywhere money nerds gathered).

It's called Modern Monetary Theory, and while its intellectual roots go back a century or so, we can start the story in the early 1990s when a hedge fund manager named Warren Mosler flew to Rome to meet with the Italian finance minister. Mosler had recently noticed that he could borrow money (Italian lira) from Italian banks and turn around and lend it to the Italian government for a higher interest rate. It was a free, guaranteed profit—as long as the Italian government didn't default on its debts. So he'd gotten a meeting with the finance minister to ensure that wouldn't happen.

Mosler had recently come to believe that most people fundamentally misunderstood how money worked. They were still stuck in a gold-standard mentality decades after the gold standard had disappeared. He pointed out that, unlike in the gold-standard world, a country that prints its own fiat currency, and borrows in that currency, never needs to default. It can always print more money to pay its debts.

Printing more money can sometimes lead to inflation, Mosler knew. But it doesn't *always* lead to inflation. He thought the essential thing for understanding an economy was not how much money the government was printing, but what was going on in the real world. Did everybody who wanted a job have a job? Were all the factories and offices operating at full capacity? Only if those things were true *and* the government kept putting more money into the economy and buying more goods and services would it start driving prices up and create inflation.

But what if the economy wasn't operating at full capacity? What if there were a lot of people who wanted a job but couldn't find one, and idle offices and factories? In that case, as the government put more money into the economy and started buying stuff, it would drive businesses to hire more workers. Prices wouldn't start rising, Mosler argued, until the economy got to full employment.

Unlike most foreign investors, Mosler wasn't trying to convince the finance minister to cut spending. He wanted to convince the minister that Italy could just print money. The minister agreed. Mosler borrowed the lira from Italian banks, then turned around and loaned it to the Italian government. The Italian government paid the money back, with interest. Mosler made millions of dollars for his hedge fund.

In the United States at the time, Congress and the president were raising taxes to fight the budget deficit. Mosler, like a lot of rich people, didn't like higher taxes. But added to this basic dislike, he now had a bigger theory of why they were unnecessary. Inflation was low; there were unemployed workers in America; rather than raising taxes, the government could simply spend more money.

The very idea that the government needs to tax citizens to spend money is backward, Mosler argued. This money that the government is collecting in taxes—where does it come from? What is the origin of a dollar? A dollar enters the world, Mosler said, when the US government buys something and the US Treasury puts dollars into the bank account of the seller. This is how dollars get out into the world in the first instance. When the government collects taxes, it is just taking back dollars it originally created to buy stuff.

He decided he had to convince powerful people that his new view of the world was right and everybody else was wrong. Through his old boss, he got a meeting with Donald Rumsfeld, who had worked for multiple presidents. Mosler flew to Chicago and, bizarrely, met with Rumsfeld in a steam room. Rumsfeld sent Mosler to Art Laffer, an economist who is most famous for arguing for lower taxes. Mosler wound up paying a colleague of Laffer's $25,000 to cowrite a paper called "Soft Currency Economics."

"In the midst of great abundance our leaders promote privation," the paper began. "We are told that we cannot afford to hire more teachers, while many teachers are unemployed. And we are told we cannot afford to give away school lunches, while surplus food goes to waste." The essential message: stop worrying about deficits all the time. The government can print and spend as much money as it wants, as long as there are people who are looking for work and unused resources exist in the economy.

Almost nobody read the paper. Mosler spent decades in the wilderness (and by wilderness, I mean the Caribbean, where he lived, in part, to avoid paying taxes). He funded a few fringe economists who were working on similar ideas, and who came up with a name for this way of looking at the world: Modern Monetary Theory, or MMT for short.

In the mid-'90s, a young economist named Stephanie Kelton studied at one of the programs funded by Mosler. She was interested but skeptical. She wanted to understand how government spending really worked. Not the theory, but the thing itself. She spent months studying the arcane details—reading Fed manuals, talking to people whose job was to move money in and out of government accounts at the Treasury Department. Where does the money come from? Where does it go? Her conclusion: the government creates dollars—puts new money into circulation—by buying stuff. It takes money out of circulation by taxing or borrowing.

For Kelton and her colleagues, the implications were huge. They shouted from the rooftops that we could worry about deficits much less, and much less often. With this abundance, they said, the government could do much more. Perhaps most important, they argued, the government could and should offer a job to any American who wanted one. If inflation starts to rise, the government can cool things off by raising taxes to take money out of the system.

In 2015, Stephanie Kelton's work caught the eye of Bernie Sanders's presidential campaign. Sanders didn't seem that interested in the details of MMT. But he liked the idea of the government being able to spend lots of money on things like a jobs guarantee. Kelton became Sanders's economic advisor and started telling reporters about MMT. The theory got another boost when Democrats won a majority in the House of Representatives two years later, and a newly elected congresswoman drew on MMT to suggest that maybe the government could start doing lots more stuff without worrying about how to pay for it.

But no politician really seemed to go all the way with MMT. That would mean not only saying the government should spend a lot more money, it would mean saying that if too much spending does create inflation, Congress should raise taxes to pull money out of the system and cool things down.

Traditional economists have questioned many of the MMT arguments. Lots of people disagree with its fundamental tenets. But that last point—the idea that we should trust Congress to fight inflation—may be the hardest part to swallow. Not for any theoretical reason. More because, *really?* Trust Congress to raise taxes when inflation starts rising? Come on.

The way we do money now is undemocratic. Politicians appoint central bankers to control a nation's (or a continent's) money. And then, to a large extent, the politicians leave the central bankers alone. If the central bankers want to create trillions of dollars and bail out shadow banks in a crisis, they can. If the central bankers want to jack up interest rates to fight inflation, they can—even if high rates mean lots of workers will lose their jobs. We have chosen to create this world. We have chosen to tie our own democratic hands and let central bankers do what they think is best.

Stephanie Kelton and the MMTers are saying that it doesn't have to be this way. Money can be more democratic. We don't have to throw people out of work to fight inflation. But to do that, we'd have to decide that we trust ourselves—that we trust our elected representatives—to control money itself.

✳ ✳ ✳

In the spring of 2020, a pandemic walloped economies around the world. More dramatically than ever before, central banks followed Walter Bagehot's advice to lend freely into a panic. In the twenty-first century, that meant trillions of dollars and euros and yen loaned to banks, and shadow banks, and ordinary businesses. That radical intervention helped to prevent a full-blown financial crisis.

But some day—maybe next week, maybe in ten years—there will be another financial crisis. And another. Technology will change and governments will change. People's beliefs about the balance between individuals and society, banks and governments, privacy and convenience, stability and growth, will all change. All of which is to say that money will change. The way we do money will look as strange to our great-great-grandchildren as a world where banks print their own paper money with pictures of Santa Claus.

Acknowledgments

Sloan Harris and Heather Karpas, my agents at ICM, told me to write a real book, and pushed me to make it good. At Hachette, Paul Whitlatch went out of his way to buy the book, Mollie Weisenfeld shepherded the manuscript along, and Lauren Marino gave a strong push at the end and made the book much better.

Planet Money is not only where I learned about money and economics; it's where I learned to tell a story. I owe a massive debt of gratitude to everyone I've worked with at NPR, but I have to single out one person in particular: David Kestenbaum. He was my mentor, my work husband through years of stories, and he remains my friend.

Bryant Urstdat helped come up with the title of this book. Keith Romer gave good notes on a messed-up draft. Alex Goldmark worked to make it easy for me to take time off from *Planet Money* to work on the book. The Brooklyn Public Library, New York Public Library, and Columbia University Libraries were essential.

My parents taught me how to think and showed me what it means to love books. My daughters are teaching me those lessons again. My wife, Alexandra Alter, read early drafts of this book and gave me guidance and wisdom about the book and everything else.

Notes

A few books helped me think broadly about how to put together a history of money. These included *A History of Money*, by Glyn Davies; *The Ascent of Money*, by Niall Ferguson; *Money*, by John Kenneth Galbraith; and *Money Changes Everything*, by William Goetzmann. I originally encountered some of the material in this book as a reporter for *Planet Money*. In the process of working on the book, I reconfirmed and extended all of my previous reporting.

Chapter 1

Mademoiselle Zélie's letter was printed as a footnote in *Traictie de la Première Invention des Monnoies de Nicole Orseme*, edited by M. L. Woloski. It was translated for me by Benoit Hochedez. The letter was made famous (among money nerds, at least) by Jevons. Details of the potlatch come from Davies.

The Caroline Humphrey quote on barter is from her article "Barter and Economic Disintegration," published in the journal *Man*. David Graeber made much of the myth of barter in *Debt: The First 5,000 Years*. Norms of gift giving and reciprocity in traditional cultures have been widely discussed, perhaps most famously in Marcel Mauss's *The Gift*. The details about different types of proto-money in different cultures come from Paul Einzig's *Primitive Money*.

The idea that writing developed from clay tokens pressed into clay balls has been developed largely by the archaeologist Denise Schmandt-Besserat and is described for a general audience in her book *How Writing Came About*. I spoke with Robert Englund, professor emeritus at UCLA, to understand Mesopotamian accounting and clay tablets. The "Abasaga" tablet is described in *Cuneiform Texts in the Metropolitan Museum of Art*.

Creators, Conquerors, and Citizens, by Robin Waterfield, provided useful details on ancient Greek history and the rise of the poleis. The archaeologist Nicholas

Cahill, who directed the dig at the former Lydian capital, spoke to me about the Lydians' invention of coins. David Schaps's *The Invention of Coinage and the Monetization of Ancient Greece* was a revelation, illuminating how coins transformed life in Greece. I spoke with Schaps to better understand a few of the points in his book, which was also the source of the Aristotle quotes.

Chapter 2

The development of coins and paper money in Sichuan was described to me in an interview by the historian Richard von Glahn. His book *The Economic History of China* was also a source.

The details of Cai Lun's invention of paper come from Mark Kurlansky's book *Paper*. Modern scholars have pointed out that, as with most inventions, the invention of paper was probably not a single epiphany, and Cai likely improved upon work others were doing.

The counterfeit currency warning is from von Glahn's paper "Re-examining the Authenticity of Song Paper Money Specimens," published in the *Journal of Song-Yuan Studies*.

The details of China's economic revolution come from Mark Elvin's book *The Pattern of the Chinese Past*. The restaurant quote comes from Nicholas Kiefer's paper "Economics and the Origin of the Restaurant," published in *Cornell Hotel and Restaurant Administration Quarterly*.

The story of the Mongols in China comes from Morris Rossabi's *Khubilai Khan: His Life and Times*, Jack Weatherford's *Genghis Khan and the Making of the Modern World*, von Glahn's *History*, and from conversations with von Glahn and Rossabi.

Kenneth Pomeranz's book *The Great Divergence* was influential on why Europe became so much richer than China in the modern era. In *The Chinese Market Economy, 1000–1500*, William Guanglin Liu provides a detailed analysis of China's economic boom and ultimate economic decline, and describes in detail the rulers' shifting views of money and markets that led to both the rise and fall of the Chinese economy.

Chapter 3

The poor quality of the coins in seventeenth-century England is discussed, among other places, in Thomas Macaulay's *History of England*, which is the source of the "wrangling" quote. Conversations with economic historians Stephen Quinn and George Selgin helped me understand the emergence of goldsmith fractional-reserve banking. Quinn's paper "Goldsmith-Banking: Mutual Acceptance and Interbanker Clearing in Restoration London," published in *Explorations in Economic History*, and Selgin's "Those Dishonest Goldsmiths," from *Financial History Review*, were also helpful. Swedish copper money is described in *The Encyclopedia of Money*, by Larry Allen, and *Money and Power*, by Gunnar Wetterberg.

The details about early Barcelona bankers come from *Money, Bank Credit, and Economic Cycles*, by Jesús Huerta de Soto. Davies was the source for much of the information about the bank run in England when King Charles decided to stop paying the debt. The quote where the treasurer of the navy worries about "notes which is now not money" comes from the British Treasury Minute Book for January 1672, which is available online, and is quoted in J. Keith Horsefield's "The Beginnings of Paper Money in England," published in the *Journal of European Economic History*.

If you want to read a biography of John Law (and who wouldn't?), I recommend Janet Gleeson's *Millionaire: The Philanderer, Gambler, and Duelist Who Invented Modern Finance*. It's fun and readable and smart and is the source of several of the biographical details of Law's life that run through chapters 3 through 7. *John Law: Economic Theorist and Policy-Maker*, by Antoin Murphy, was also a major source for these chapters and is especially strong on Law's writing and thinking about money and economics. Law's story is also discussed at length in Ferguson, Galbraith, and Davies.

Chapter 4

The history and math of the problem of the points is described in detail by Keith Devlin in his book *The Unfinished Game*.

Ian Hacking's *The Emergence of Probability* helped me think about the radical transformation in thought that came with the rise of probability and is the source of the knucklebone information. Peter Bernstein's *Against the Gods* had useful narrative detail about Pascal and Halley.

Halley's paper was called "An Estimate of the Degrees of the Mortality of Mankind; drawn from curious Tables of the Births and Funerals at the City of Breslaw; with an Attempt to ascertain the Price of Annuities upon Lives."

It was published in the *Philosophical Transactions of the Royal Society*. James Ciecka's "Edmond Halley's Life Table and Its Uses," published in the *Journal of Legal Economics*, was a useful guide.

The figures from Wallace and Webster's life insurance fund are from "Early Actuarial Work in Eighteenth-Century Scotland," by J. B. Dow, published in the *Transactions of the Faculty of Actuaries*. The Wallace and Webster story is well told by Ferguson.

Chapter 5

Matt Levine writes for Bloomberg. The quote about finance as time travel comes from his "Money Stuff" newsletter, which is great.

The most important source for this chapter was *The World's First Stock Exchange*, by Lodewijk Petram. The book includes a lucid narrative of the VOC, the Amsterdam Stock Exchange, and the work of Isaac Le Maire. Also useful were "The Formative Years of the Modern Corporation: The Dutch East India Company VOC, 1602–1623," from the *Journal of Economic History*, by Oscar Gelderblom, Abe de Jong, and Joost Jonker; and "Isaac Le Maire and the Share Trading of the Dutch East India Company," by J. G. van Dillen, as translated by Asha Majithia and published in *Pioneers of Financial Economics*, Volume 1.

Joseph de la Vega, author of *Confusion of Confusions*, was born in Spain. His book was originally published in Spanish as *Confusion de Confusiones*.

Chapter 6

Details on Amsterdam's public bank come mainly from "Early Public Banks," a Federal Reserve Bank of Chicago working paper by William Roberds and François R. Velde, and from my interview with Velde.

Law's "Money and Trade Considered" is discussed at length in Murphy's biography of Law. His wanderings through Europe and rise in France are described by Gleeson and Murphy. The *Memoirs* of Duc de Saint-Simon, Volume 3, translated by Lucy Norton, are a great source of details about the Duke of Orléans's debauched style, as well as Law's rise through Parisian society.

Details about the creation of the Bank of England come from *Till Time's Last Sand: A History of the Bank of England, 1694–2013*, by David Kynaston. The magazine that reported the Regent's deposit in John Law's bank was the *Gazette de la Régence*, as quoted in Gleeson.

Chapter 7

The key sources for this chapter are Gleeson; Murphy; "John Law's System," published by François Velde in the *American Economic Review*; and my interview with Velde.

The quote from the Regent's mother about tobacco is from Gleeson. The description of supplicants coming down Law's chimney comes from Saint-Simon. The quote from Defoe is from *John Law and the Mississippi Scheme*, an anthology of Defoe's writings on Law.

The quote from the clerk at the British embassy describing the mania comes from Murphy, as does the quote from the French government thanking Law.

The transportation of criminals to the Mississippi colony is described in *Louisiana and the Gulf South Frontier, 1500–1821*, by F. Todd Smith. Information on inflation comes from "Prices and Wages at Paris Under John Law's System," by Earl J. Hamilton, published in the *Quarterly Journal of Economics*. The Saint-Simon quote comes from his *Memoirs*.

Gleeson and Murphy are the key sources for the details of John Law's life after the collapse.

Chapter 8

Nordhaus's paper on the history of light was called "Do Real-Output and Real-Wage Measures Capture Reality? The History of Lighting Suggests Not." It was published in a collection called *The Economics of New Goods*. In the paper, he not only analyzed the history of light, he also concluded that economists had been underestimating the gains in lighting technology, and as a result had underestimated the extent to which people had become richer over time.

Many of the details about Nordhaus's investigation come from a personal interview. Some of the figures presented in the chapter were calculated by Nordhaus at my request (similar figures are presented in Nordhaus's paper, but in a more complicated way).

Details on ways people made artificial light, and on people locking themselves in their houses overnight, come from *Brilliant*, by Jane Brox. Information on

Thomas Edison comes from *Brilliant* and from *The Edison Papers*, hosted online by Rutgers University. The *New York Times* article about health inspectors and Edison's smokestacks was quoted in *Brilliant* and was from an article published on January 17, 1911.

Chapter 9

Many of the narrative details about the Luddites come from *The Making of the English Working Class*, by E. P. Thompson. *Rebels Against the Future*, by Kirkpatrick Sale, was also a useful source.

Marc Andreessen published "Why Software Is Eating the World" as an op-ed in the *Wall Street Journal*.

The story about Roper selling his invention for £5 comes from *The Strutts and the Arkwrights, 1758–1830*, by R. S. Fitton and Alfred P. Wadsworth.

Quotes from Luddite letters come from *Writings of the Luddites*, edited by Kevin Binfield. I also interviewed Binfield to get an overview of the era.

Data on workers' wages in this era, how they were an incentive for mechanization, and how they stagnated after mechanization, come from Robert Allen's *The British Industrial Revolution in Global Perspective* and Allen's "Engels' Pause: Technical Change, Capital Accumulation, and Inequality in the British Industrial Revolution," from *Explorations in Economic History*.

Eric Hobsbawm called the Luddite attacks "collective bargaining by riot." The economic historian Joel Mokyr provided useful details about the Luddites in an interview.

Chapter 10

Hume's *Political Discourses* was published in 1752. The chapter on trade is "Of the Balance of Trade." *The Infidel and the Professor*, by Dennis C. Rasmussen, helped me understand Hume's work and, especially, Hume's influence on Adam Smith.

Britain's unintentional creation of the gold standard is described in Davies. Galbraith is good on the rise of the free silver movement in the United States. Details on William Jennings Bryan come from *A Godly Hero: The Life of William Jennings Bryan*, by Michael Kazin. The rock critic Greil Marcus used the phrases "anxiety and success" and "terror and deliverance" in *Bob Dylan by Greil Marcus*.

McKinley's speech is described in "Playing to the Press in McKinley's Front Porch Campaign," by William Harpine, published in *Rhetoric Society Quarterly*. The full speech was reported in the *Indianapolis Journal* under the headline "Money is the Issue."

The key sources on Irving Fisher are *My Father, Irving Fisher*, by Irving Norton Fisher, and *Irving Fisher: A Biography*, by Robert Loring Allen. More recently, Sylvia Nassar wrote extensively about Fisher in her excellent book *Grand Pursuit: The Story of Economic Genius*. I also relied on Fisher's own writings, especially *The Money Illusion, Stabilizing the Dollar*, and *Stable Money*.

Domestic box office figures come from Box Office Mojo. Inflation calculations were made with the Bureau of Labor Statistics' CPI Inflation Calculator.

Chapter 11

Thomas Govan's *Nicholas Biddle* is the standard biography of Biddle and the source for details on his early life. In describing Biddle's work running the Bank of the United States, I relied largely on Jane Knodell's *The Second Bank of the United States* and on an interview I did with Knodell. Richard Sylla, of NYU, called Biddle the "world's first self-conscious central banker" in an interview with the Minneapolis Fed.

Details about Andrew Jackson's life come from Arthur Schlesinger Jr.'s *The Age of Jackson*, Jon Meacham's *American Lion*, and *Andrew Jackson*, by H. W. Brands. Taney's complaints about Biddle are from Taney's "Bank War Manuscript."

Bray Hammond's *Banks and Politics in America: From the Revolution to the Civil War* was a key source for the free banking era. The quote about coins that "flew about the country with the celerity of magic" is from a Michigan bank commissioners' report from 1839 and is quoted in Galbraith.

The number of banknotes in circulation comes from "Our Abominable Currency System," published in the *Chicago Tribune* on February 13, 1863. In an interview, Matthew Jaremski mentioned the Santa Claus note as a particularly delightful example of a banknote of the era. I found an example of a Santa Claus note in Thompson's 1859 *Bank Note Descriptive List, Supplementary to Thompson's Bank Note & Commercial Reporter*.

The case in which a court said the right to deal in money should be as free as the right to deal in wheat or cotton was *Warner v. Beers*, in 1840. The quote about the traveler having to constantly change money is from *Letters of Lowndes*. One of the important early papers in rethinking the free banking era was "The Free Banking Era: A Reexamination," by Hugh Rockoff, published in the *Journal of Money, Credit and Banking*. "Do Economists Reach a Conclusion on Free Banking Episodes?" by Rockoff and Ignacio Briones, published in *Econ Journal Watch*, is a good overview of the literature. The quote from Bagehot is from his book *Lombard Street*, still an essential source on the function of central banks during crises.

Roger Lowenstein's *America's Bank: The Epic Struggle to Create the Federal Reserve* is a comprehensive account of the creation of the Fed and the source for many of the details about the origins of the Fed.

The quote about people blaming the wily practices of Wall Street is from Paul Warburg's *The Federal Reserve System: Its Origin and Growth*. Gary Gorton wrote that if Wall Street greed caused financial crises, we'd have a crisis every week.

The quote about meeting in secret on the train car came from Frank A. Vanderlip, president of the National City Bank, who described the experience in the *Saturday Evening Post*.

The details of how the Fed emerged after the bankers came back from Jekyll Island come from Lowenstein.

Chapter 12

Lords of Finance, by Liaquat Ahamed, is brilliant and insightful and more delightful than a book about central bankers and the Great Depression has any right to be. It is an essential source for this chapter.

The other essential source is *A Monetary History of the United States, 1867–1960*, by Milton Friedman and Anna Schwartz, who described in great detail everything the Federal Reserve banks did during this period, and who changed the way economists understand the Great Depression.

"The self-fulfilling prophecy" was coined in an article of the same name, published in *The Antioch Review* by Robert K. Merton. The 2012 survey of economists' views on the gold standard was conducted by the IGM Forum at the University of Chicago Booth School of Business. Hoover's "forced off the gold standard...means chaos" quote comes from a campaign speech in Des Moines, Iowa, on October 4, 1932.

Arthur Schlesinger Jr.'s "pseudo-respectability" quote is from his book *The Coming of the New Deal, 1933–1935*. Warren's trip on a little plane to see Roosevelt is described in *The Money Makers*, by Eric Rauchway. Details on the bartering that emerged as money disappeared come from Ahamed.

The Woodin quote is from *One Nation Under Gold*, by James Ledbetter. The Roosevelt quote is from the official transcript of his press conference on March 8, 1933.

A firsthand account of the "end of Western Civilization" scene, when Roosevelt told his advisors he was taking the United States off the gold standard, comes from Raymond Moley's *After Seven Years*. The scene is also described in Rauchway. Irving Fisher's letter to his wife is quoted in *My Father, Irving Fisher*.

Data on recoveries in prices, employment, and incomes in 1933 come from the St. Louis Fed. A key work on how the gold standard caused a global depression, and how leaving the gold standard was essential to turning the economy around, is *Golden Fetters*, by Barry Eichengreen. "The Gold Standard and the Great Depression," by Eichengreen and Peter Temin, published in *Contemporary European History*, is a useful analysis of how "the mentality of the gold standard" transformed an ordinary economic contraction into the Great Depression.

Roosevelt's letter to a Harvard professor is quoted in Schlesinger.

Chapter 13

The idea that a shadow bank run was at the heart of the financial crisis of 2008 was largely developed by Gary Gorton, a Yale economist (who also worked for AIG, which was bailed out during the crisis by the federal government). Gorton's book *Misunderstanding Financial Crises* is a good overview.

The story of Bruce Bent's early life, and his development of the money-market mutual fund, comes largely from an interview I conducted with Bent and his son, Bruce Bent II.

Some details of the early growth of the Reserve Fund come from the *Wall Street Journal* obituary of Henry Brown, "Co-Inventor of Money-Market Account Helped Serve Small Investors' Interest," by Stephen Miller.

Figures on the growth of money-market funds and their role in buying commercial paper come from "The Road to Repeal of the Glass-Steagall Act," by

Arthur Wilmarth, published in the *Wake Forest Journal of Business and Intellectual Property Law*, and "The Evolution of the U.S. Commercial Paper Market Since 1980," by Mitchell A. Post, published in the *Federal Reserve Bulletin*. Citi's invention of asset-backed commercial paper is described in *The Growth of Shadow Banking*, by Matthias Thiemann.

Bent's 2001 "garbage" quote about commercial paper was cited by the 2008 *Wall Street Journal* article "A Money-Fund Manager's Fateful Shift," by Steve Stecklow and Diya Gullapalli, which traced Bent's move into commercial paper. The "prudent rather than plain" quote from Bent II is from the Nov. 6, 2000, *Wall Street Journal* article "Money-Market Funds Suit Many Investors, But Proud Creator Frets About Extra Risk," by Bridget O'Brian.

The writings of Zoltan Pozsar are an excellent source on the rise of institutional pools of money. See, for example, his *Federal Reserve Bank of New York Staff Report* "Shadow Banking," coauthored with Tobias Adrian, Adam Ashcraft, and Hayley Boesky. Pozsar also talked me through his ideas in an interview.

McCulley coined the term "shadow banking" at the Federal Reserve's Jackson Hole conference in 2007. He later described that moment in an April 2010 speech titled "After the Crisis: Planning a New Financial Structure Learning from the Bank of Dad," the transcript of which is posted on PIMCO's website.

The Ricks quote is from his book *The Money Problem: Rethinking Financial Regulation*. Ricks also spoke with me in an interview.

The details on the fall of Bear Stearns come from the *Financial Crisis Inquiry Report*, published by the Financial Crisis Inquiry Commission. Bear Stearns and Lehman Brothers were both largely borrowing in the repo market.

The "sound night's sleep" quote from Bent is from the *Wall Street Journal* article "Father of Money Funds Raps His Creation," by Daisy Maxey. The annual report was published on May 31, 2008.

Details of what happened at the Primary Fund the week of Sept. 15, 2008, come from a lawsuit the Securities and Exchange Commission filed in 2009 against Bruce Bent, Bruce Bent II, the Reserve Primary Fund, and its parent company. The jury cleared the Bents of fraud charges. They found that Bent II was liable for one claim of negligence, and the parent company was found to have made fraudulent statements. Direct quotes of conversations come from transcripts of phone calls that were introduced into the court record as part of the case. The lawyer who worked at the New York Fed during the crisis spoke with me in an interview.

The quotes from President Bush are from the official transcript of his Sept. 19, 2008, speech, "Remarks on the National Economy."

The Group of Thirty report was "Financial Reform: A Framework for Financial Stability." The industry report that argued against fundamental change was the "Report of the Money Market Working Group" of the Investment Company Institute.

The Sheila Bair quote is from the *Wall Street Journal* article "Why the Fed Had to Backstop Money-Market Funds, Again," by Paul Kiernan, Andrew Ackerman, and Dave Michaels.

Chapter 14

The Euro, by David Marsh, is an excellent book-length treatment of the origins of the euro. It is a key source for this chapter, including for most of the early exchanges between European leaders. The German magazine *Der Spiegel's* article "Was the Deutsche Mark Sacrificed for Reunification?" was also an important source. Pohl and his colleagues argued for "comprehensive political union" in the "Monthly Report of the Deutsche Bundesbank, October 1990." The Frankfurt fireworks at the introduction of the euro were described in the *Los Angeles Times* article "It's Happy New Euro for a Continent," by Carol J. Williams.

Fast economic growth in peripheral euro-area countries was noted in the European Commission's *Annual Report on the Euro Area 2007*. George Papandreou is the Greek prime minister who disclosed that the deficit was 12 percent. Jean-Claude Juncker is the one who said "the game is over" after Greek statistics were found out.

The details about government spending and tax evasion in Greece come from *Greece's 'Odious' Debt*, by Jason Manolopoulos. The "stupid to finance profligacy" quote from Martin Wolf appears in his book *The Shifts and the Shocks*. "A look back: what Eurozone 'risk sharing' actually meant," by Marcello Minenna, published online by the *Financial Times*, shows German bank lending to Greece, Spain, and other eurozone countries. The German trade surplus with the rest of the eurozone is described in "The German trade surplus may widen with the euro area recovery," published by the think tank Bruegel. Data on unemployment rates and economic growth come from the St. Louis Fed. Federal versus state tax data come from the Tax Policy Center Briefing Book. Retirement age in Greece and Germany was discussed in the *Economist* article "What Makes Germans So Very Cross About Greece?" The "political union" quote from Kohl is from *The Birth of the Euro*, by Otmar Issing.

The "Titanic" quote from the Spanish foreign minister was reported in the *Guardian* article "Spain Issues Dramatic Messages of Impending Eurozone Doom," by Giles Tremlett. The biographical details about Mario Draghi, and details surrounding his "whatever it takes" speech, come from the Bloomberg News story "3 Words and $3 Trillion: The Inside Story of How Mario Draghi Saved the Euro," by Jana Randow and Alessandro Speciale.

Chapter 15

Digital Gold, by Nathaniel Popper, and *The Age of Cryptocurrency*, by Paul Vigna and Michael J. Casey, are useful overviews of the story of bitcoin and cryptocurrency. *This Machine Kills Secrets*, by Andy Greenberg, is a good telling of the cypherpunk story.

David Chaum published "Security Without Identification: Transaction Systems to Make Big Brother Obsolete" in *Communications of the ACM*. Chaum described his early life to me in a phone interview. The patent I quote from is for a "Cryptographic identification, financial transaction, and credential device."

The *Wired* quote is from "E-Money (That's What I Want)," by Steven Levy. The *New York Times Magazine* quote is from "Dead as a Dollar," by James Gleick. Citibank's e-money program, and the international spread of Digi-Cash, are described in *The Age of Cryptocurrency*. The Greenspan quote is from a 1997 speech, "Privacy in the Information Age."

Timothy May described his discovery of Chaum's work, and his role in creating the cypherpunks, in an interview with me. Some cypherpunk details come from *This Machine Kills Secrets*, and from *The Dark Net*, by Jamie Bartlett.

Back's 1997 email is archived at hashcash.org. "Pricing via Processing, or Combatting Junk Mail" was published in the proceedings of the Crypto '92 conference. Wei Dai's b-money proposal is archived at weidai.com. The email from Satoshi Nakamoto to Wei Dai is at nakamotostudies.org. The original bitcoin paper is known as the "Bitcoin Whitepaper" and is available at bitcoin .org, among many other places. The 2009 Nakamoto messages are at nakamo toinstitute.org. The Laszlo pizza post was (and is) at bitcointalk.org. The buyer of the pizza was profiled by Mark Molloy in a *Telegraph* article headlined "The inside story behind the famous 2010 bitcoin pizza purchase today worth $83m."

The quotes from the Dread Pirate Roberts are from "Collected Quotations of the Dread Pirate Roberts, Founder of Underground Drug Site Silk Road and Radical Libertarian," published in *Forbes*. The drug listings from the Silk Road are from a Sept. 27, 2013, complaint filed in *United States v. Ross William Ulbricht, aka Dread Pirate Roberts*. The quote from Ulbricht's sentencing is from the *Wired* story "Silk Road Creator Ross Ulbricht Sentenced to Life in Prison," by Andy Greenberg.

The Senate hearing was called "Beyond Silk Road: Potential Risks, Threats, and Promises of Virtual Currencies." Testimony is posted on the committee's website. The *Washington Post* story "This Senate hearing is a bitcoin lovefest" was by Timothy B. Lee. The *Wall Street Journal* story quoting the venture capitalist was "Bitcoin Startups Begin to Attract Real Cash," by Sarah E. Needleman and Spencer E. Ante. Visa's transaction capacity comes from Visa's website. The Gavin Andresen quote is from my interview with Andresen. Bitcoin exchange rates are from coindesk.com.

Conclusion

The Kenyan mobile-money-by-text system was M-Pesa. The figure for Alipay was cited by the Reuters story "China's Ant aims for $200 bln price tag in private share sales," by Julie Zhu, Kane Wu, and Zhang Yan. Figures for the amount of cash in circulation, and the denominations, come from the Federal Reserve. Ken Rogoff argued for getting rid of big bills in his book *The Curse of Cash*.

The Swedish cash heist was described in detail in the *Atavist Magazine* article "Lifted," by Evan Ratliff. Figures for declining cash use in Sweden come from the Riksbank report "Payments in Sweden 2019." The quote from the Swedish National Pensioners' Association is from "Sweden's Push to Get Rid of Cash Has Some Saying, 'Not So Fast,'" a *New York Times* article by Liz Alderman.

The "chief loose screw" quote comes from "A Program for Monetary Reform," a report written by Irving Fisher and several other economists in 1939. Milton Friedman discussed full-reserve banking in *A Program for Monetary Stability*. The John Cochrane quote is from an interview with me. The "worst is the one we have today" quote is from Mervyn King's 2010 speech "Banking—from Bagehot to Basel, and Back Again."

Representative Ocasio-Cortez supported MMT in the *Business Insider* article "Alexandria Ocasio-Cortez says the theory that deficit spending is good for the economy should 'absolutely' be part of the conversation," by Eliza Relman. Stephanie Kelton and Warren Mosler told me their stories in phone interviews. Mosler's ideas are also described in *Seven Deadly Innocent Frauds of Economic Policy*.

Index

duel, Law and Wilson, 32–33
Dutch, financing spice trade, 45, 46
    See also Amsterdam
Dutch East India Company. *See*
    VOC (Vereenigde Oostindische
    Compagnie)
Dwork, Cynthia, 195

economic benefits of euro, 174–175
economic collapse of France at end of
    Louis XIV's reign, 59
economic growth, technological
    improvement and, 21–22, 23
economic revolution, money and
    Chinese, 17–19, 23
Economist magazine, 129, 191
Edison, Thomas, 82–84
Edison Electric Light Company, 83–84
e-krona, 217
electricity, to make light, 82–84
"Electronic Cash Without a Trusted
    Third Party" (Nakamoto), 198
Electronic Monetary System, 190, 191
electrum, 9
email spam, trying to solve, 195
emergency banking law (US), 143–144
England
    determining worth of silver coins in
        seventeenth-century, 27–28
    goldsmiths becoming bankers in, 25,
        28–30
    Industrial Revolution, 21, 90–97
    raising money in, 59–61
    See also Bank of England; Britain;
        Parliament
English East India Company, 47
"An Estimate of the Degrees of the
    Mortality of Mankind, drawn
    from curious Tables of the
    Birth and Funerals at the City
    of Breslau: with an Attempt to
    ascertain the Price of Annuities
    upon Lives" (Halley), 40–41

euro, 169–185
    Draghi instilling trust and
        preservation of, 184–185
    economic problems created by
        lack of unified political system,
        181–183
    equalization of access to finance
        among countries and, 174
    initial economic benefits of,
        174–175
    low deficits and low inflation as
        conditions of entry into, 173,
        174
    as miracle, 173–175
    Mitterand and, 170–171, 172
    Pöhl's demands for, 173
    pressure on Germany to accept,
        170–173
    as trap, 175–179
European Central Bank (ECB), 173
    bailout for Greece, Portugal, and
        Ireland, 182
    Draghi and, 183–185
    as lender of last resort, 183
    raising interest rates in
        response to sustained financial
        crisis, 182
European Commission, 182
European financial crisis
    depth and length of, 179
    Greece and, 175–179
    See also euro
executive order 6102, 145–146
Expedia, 89

farmers
    gold standard and, 106, 108–109
    in revolt during Great Depression,
        144
federal government (US)
    aid to states after financial crisis,
        180–181
    interest in digital cash, 190

John Law's System. *See* Mississippi
    Bubble
JPMorgan Chase, purchase of Bear
    Stearns, 160

Kayak, 89
Kelton, Stephanie, 224–226
kerosene, as new fuel source for light,
    81–82, 85, 86
Keynes, John Maynard, 141
Köhl, Helmut
    on need for political union for
        monetary union to work, 181
    pressure to accept single European
        currency, 170–171, 172
Kublai Khan, 19–20

Laffer, Art, 223
Law, John, 26
    acquisition of right to trade tobacco
        in France, 65
    appointed Controller-General of
        Finances for France, 67–68
    creation of Banque Générale, 61–62
    desire for too much power, 73
    Dutch artist's cartoon of Mississippi
        Bubble, 72
    early life and escape from prison,
        31–33
    finding out all the chances of the
        dice, 39
    as the French economy, 67
    friendship with Duke of Orléans,
        58–59
    gambling and, 35
    introduction of income tax in
        France, 66
    life after fleeing France, 71
    Mississippi Company and, 63–64
    move to Paris, 58
    paper money and, 61, 64, 70–71
    plan to create financial system in
        France, 61
    plan to return to Scotland and
        create financial system, 56–57
    return to European wandering,
        57–58
    right to collect taxes on behalf of
        French king, 66
    settlement of area west of
        Mississippi River and, 69
    wealth of, 58, 67
ledger money, trackable, 188
Lehman Brothers
    debt to Reserve Fund, 162–164
    filing for bankruptcy, 160–161
Le Maire, Isaac, 49–53
lenders, 219–220
Levine, Matt, 46
Lewis and Clark, 121
Life Extension Institute, 111
life insurance, 42
light
    history of price of artificial, 77–82,
        85–88
    invention of lightbulb, 82–84
    making, 78–79
    sources of, 78–79
lightbulb
    cost of light, 85–88
    invention of, 82–84
limited liability corporation (LLC),
    83
Lincoln, Abraham, 128
Lindberg, Charles, 142
Louis XIV, 58
Louis XV, 59
"Love-Letters Between a Certain Late
    Nobleman and the Famous Mr.
    Wilson" (pamphlet), 32
Ludd, Edward "Ned," invention of, 93
Luddites, 90–97
Lydia, invention of coins in, 9

Macaulay, Thomas, 27
mace, 52

Reserve Association of the United
  States, 132
reserve associations, 132
Reserve Fund (Reserve Primary Fund)
  buying commercial paper, 161–162
  conservative investment strategy,
    153–154, 155, 156
  creation of, 155
  end of, 166
  run on, 162–164
Ricks, Morgan, 159
Riksbank, 217
ritual sacrifice, rules for, 5
Rogoff, Ken, 215–216
Roosevelt, Franklin Delano, 126
  executive order 6102, 145–146
  gold standard and, 143, 145–146, 148
  promise of "sound money," 141
  radio address on banks and money,
    144–145
  Warren and, 142–143
Royal Mint (France), 61, 65
Rumsfeld, Donald, 223

Saint-Simon (duke), 72–73
St. Mondays, 91, 96
Sanders, Bernie, 225
saving, 46
Schaps, David, 11
Schlesinger, Arthur, Jr., 141
Schwartz, Anna, 140
science, practical applications of, 81
scientific revolution, 21
Scotland, Law's return to, 56–57
Scottish Ministers' Widows' Fund, 42
Second Bank of the United States,
    119–120
  Jackson and, 121–122
Securities and Exchange Commission
    (SEC), 155
self-fulfilling prophecy, 136
Senate hearing on bitcoin, 206
shadow banking, 158–161

creating real money, 159
reinvention of, 220
run on, 157–158, 159–161
safety net for, 166
shadow money is real money,
    164–166
shares at set price in mutual fund, 154
shearing frames, Luddites attack on,
    95–96
Shirley, Judith, 60
shitcoins, 209
short, stock, 49–53
Silicon Valley, bitcoin and, 206
Silk Road, 205–206
silver
  abandoned as money, 104
  as money-ish in Mesopotamia, 7
silver coins, 10, 59, 61, 70, 71
  deciding worth of in seventeenth-
    century England, 27–28
  setting value for, 104
  trading them for gold in Paris or
    Amsterdam, 28
silverites, 106, 108–109, 110
silver reserves, state banks and, 125
Smith, Adam, 4, 103
social insurance, 42–43
"Soft Currency Economics" (Mosler),
    223–224
software, effects of business, 89–90
Spain, worry about lending to, 176,
    177, 182–183
Spice Islands, European trade with, 45,
    46–47
Stable Money Association, 141
Stable Money League, 114–115
state banking regulator, 124
state banks, 119
  printing money, 124–128
  regulation of, 119–120
  running wild, 123
  scandals and, 124, 125
  tax on paper money issued by, 128